Adolf Hitler

These and other titles are included in The Importance
Of biography series:

Alexander the Great	Adolf Hitler
Muhammad Ali	Harry Houdini
Louis Armstrong	Thomas Jefferson
Clara Barton	Chief Joseph
Napoleon Bonaparte	Malcolm X
Rachel Carson	Margaret Mead
Charlie Chaplin	Michelangelo
Cesar Chavez	Wolfgang Amadeus Mozart
Winston Churchill	Sir Isaac Newton
Cleopatra	Richard M. Nixon
Christopher Columbus	Georgia O'Keeffe
Hernando Cortes	Louis Pasteur
Marie Curie	Pablo Picasso
Amelia Earhart	Jackie Robinson
Thomas Edison	Anwar Sadat
Albert Einstein	Margaret Sanger
Duke Ellington	Oskar Schindler
Dian Fossey	John Steinbeck
Benjamin Franklin	Jim Thorpe
Galileo Galilei	Mark Twain
Martha Graham	Pancho Villa
Stephen Hawking	H. G. Wells
Jim Henson	

Adolf Hitler

by
Eleanor H. Ayer

Lucent Books, P.O. Box 289011, San Diego, CA 92198-9011

Library of Congress Cataloging-in-Publication Data

Ayer, Eleanor H.
   Adolf Hitler / by Eleanor H. Ayer.
       p. cm.—(The importance of)
   Includes bibliographical references and index.
   ISBN 1-56006-072-7
   1. Hitler, Adolf, 1889–1945—Juvenile literature.
   2. Heads of state—Germany—Biography—Juvenile literature.
   3. Germany—History—1933-1945—Juvenile literature.
   4. National socialism. [1. Hitler, Adolf, 1889-1945.   2. Heads
   of state.   3. Germany—History—1933-1945.   4. National
   socialism.]   I. Title.   II. Series.
   DD247.H5A97   1996
   943.086'092—dc20   95-1277
   [B]   CIP
                                                              AC

Contents

Foreword

THE IMPORTANCE OF biography series deals with individuals who have made a unique contribution to history. The editors of the series have deliberately chosen to cast a wide net and include people from all fields of endeavor. Individuals from politics, music, art, literature, philosophy, science, sports, and religion are all represented. In addition, the editors did not restrict the series to individuals whose accomplishments have helped change the course of history. Of necessity, this criterion would have eliminated many whose contribution was great, though limited. Charles Darwin, for example, was responsible for radically altering the scientific view of the natural history of the world. His achievements continue to impact the study of science today. Others, such as Chief Joseph of the Nez Percé, played a pivotal role in the history of their own people. While Joseph's influence does not extend much beyond the Nez Percé, his nonviolent resistance to white expansion and his continuing role in protecting his tribe and his homeland remain an inspiration to all.

These biographies are more than factual chronicles. Each volume attempts to emphasize an individual's contributions both in his or her own time and for posterity. For example, the voyages of Christopher Columbus opened the way to European colonization of the New World. Unquestionably, his encounter with the New World brought monumental changes to both Europe and the Americas in his day. Today, however, the broader impact of Columbus's voyages is being critically scrutinized. *Christopher Columbus,* as well as every biography in The Importance Of series, includes and evaluates the most recent scholarship available on each subject.

Each author includes a wide variety of primary and secondary source quotations to document and substantiate his or her work. All quotes are footnoted to show readers exactly how and where biographers derive their information, as well as provide stepping stones to further research. These quotations enliven the text by giving readers eyewitness views of the life and times of each individual covered in The Importance Of series.

Finally, each volume is enhanced by photographs, bibliographies, chronologies, and comprehensive indexes. For both the casual reader and the student engaged in research, The Importance Of biographies will be a fascinating adventure into the lives of people who have helped shape humanity's past and present, and who will continue to shape its future.

IMPORTANT DATES IN THE LIFE OF ADOLF HITLER

1889
Adolf Hitler is born April 20 in Braunau-am-Inn, Austria.

1903
Becomes male head of the house at age thirteen, when father Alois dies.

1905
Meets August Kubizek, friend of his teenage years.

1907
Is refused admission to the General Painting School of the Vienna Academy of Fine Arts, Austria; Klara, Adolf's mother, dies of cancer.

1913
Moves from Vienna to Munich, Germany.

1914
World War I begins; Hitler joins the Bavarian army.

1918
Blinded by poison gas while fighting in Belgium; while hospitalized, learns of Germany's defeat in World War I.

1920
Joins the German Workers' Party (DAP).

1921
Becomes president of DAP.

1923
Carries out Munich Beer Hall Putsch; is arrested and sentenced to prison.

1924
Writes *Mein Kampf* while serving time in prison.

1931
Hitler's niece, Geli Raubal, is found shot to death in his apartment.

1933
Adolf Hitler becomes chancellor of Germany on January 30; on April 1 orders boycott of Jewish businesses throughout Germany.

1934
The Röhm Purge, or the Night of the Long Knives, emasculates the SA.

1935
The Nuremberg Laws, severely limiting rights of German Jews, go into effect.

1936
On March 7 Hitler orders his army to occupy the Rhineland, an area of Germany that had been occupied by France since the end of World War I.

1938
German troops invade Austria on March 12, accomplishing the *Anschluss*—reunification of the Germanic peoples; German troops invade the Sudetenland in Czechoslovakia on October 1; Kristallnacht, "Night of the Broken Glass," on November 9 and 10 results in large-scale, Nazi-directed violence against German Jews.

1939
On March 15, German troops march into Czechoslovakia, overtaking the remainder of the country; Germany attacks Poland on September 1; World War II begins.

1940
RAF planes overpower the Luftwaffe during Battle of Britain, prompting Hitler to postpone his planned invasion of Great Britain.

1941
Operation Barbarossa, the German invasion of the Soviet Union, begins on June 22.

1942
The Wannsee Conference to draw up plans for the Final Solution to the Jewish Question is held near Berlin on January 20.

1943
German troops surrender at Stalingrad in February.

1944
The D day invasion of Europe by Allied troops begins on June 6; Claus von Stauffenberg and other officers are unsuccessful in their attempt to assassinate Hitler on July 20; Hitler orders the Ardennes Offensive on December 16, Germany's last major attack of the war, known later as the Battle of the Bulge.

1945
Auschwitz, largest of the Nazi concentration camps, is liberated on January 27 by the Russian army; Hitler makes his last public appearance on April 20, speaking to a group of Hitler Youth members; marries his longtime mistress, Eva Braun, on April 29; Hitler and Eva Braun commit suicide in their underground bunker in Berlin on April 30; German troops surrender to Allied forces on May 7; World War II in Europe is over.

"You, My Youth"

Adolf Hitler in Alfons Heck,
A Child of Hitler

The ancient city of Nuremberg, Germany, has long been the scene of grand celebrations. Here, surrounded by the dense forests of Bavaria, generations of Germanic people have held festivals, parades, and rallies to honor their heritage. Nuremberg is the soul of Germany; all that is strong, powerful, and proud in German history is reflected in this eleventh-century city. The wall that encloses the city center dates from the Middle Ages, as do the massive stone castles perched on nearby hillsides. Inside the wall stand ancient Gothic cathedrals, their pointed spires piercing the sky. A medieval marketplace, ornate fountains, and other awesome architectural landmarks make this city a stage where all of Germany can perform.

A Hero of the People

Early in the twentieth-century, a new cast of characters took the stage. They were the Nazis, under Adolf Hitler. This bold band of upstarts arrived at a time when Germany's image lay at an all-time low. Devastated by their defeat in World War I, the German people were looking for a hero—a leader who could restore pride in

themselves and in their country. They found that person in Adolf Hitler.

Although not a German by birth, Hitler harbored a fierce love for his adopted homeland. There had been a time in history when Austria, Germany, and surrounding countries of Europe all had been one. Hitler intended to bring

Hitler surveys troops during the 1933 Nazi rally in Nuremberg. Staged in this ancient German city, the week-long rallies were grand, awe-inspiring celebrations of Nazi power and might.

back that time. His dream was to reunite the Germanic people into a mighty empire once again.

Each year after beginning his rise to power, Hitler staged a rally in the proud old city of Nuremberg. This rally, the *Reichsparteitag*, was "the annual high mass of the Nazis," explained one young follower. "All of Germany went on a seven-day [patriotic] binge that inspired the nation and stunned the rest of the world." Attending this "feverish, week-long high that lasted into one's dreams,"[1] were thousands of believers: high-ranking Nazis, lower-level Nazi Party members, and hordes of clean-cut young Germans who belonged to the Hitler Youth, the national organization of young people ages ten to eighteen.

Hitler Youth members worshiped their führer, or leader, Adolf Hitler, and their adoration was returned by him. Repeatedly he told his young followers that they held the key to Germany's glorious future. "There was never a single rally without the Hitler Youth," recalled one member. "We were the icing on the cake."[2] So strongly did these young people believe in Hitler that they were ready to do anything for him—even die.

Saturday, September 10, was the Day of the Hitler Youth at the 1938 Nuremberg *Reichsparteitag*. There, in the great stadium, lined up row on row, stood eighty thousand uniformed members of the Hitler Youth, feet apart, left hands on their belts. Directly before them were two huge grandstands, where enormous granite swastikas —symbols of the Nazi Party—were displayed below the German eagle. As the order *"Achtung!"* ("Attention!") sounded through the stadium, the Hitler Youth "froze to quivering attention,"[3] awaiting the appearance of the man who had be-come their god. Alfons Heck, a member of the Jungvolk, the junior branch of the Hitler Youth, stood in the first row, just a few feet from the speaker's platform.

When Hitler finally appeared, we greeted him with a thundering, triple *"Sieg Heil,"* and it took all of our discipline to end it there, as we had been instructed. Hitler, the superb actor he was, always began his speeches quietly, almost conversationally man to man. He then increased both tempo and volume steadily. It was a sure-fire method. . . . We never had a chance. I am sure none of us in that audience took our eyes off him.[4]

As Hitler spoke, his voice rose and fell like ocean waves, building each time to a higher crest, until it took on a rasping, yet strangely appealing quality. With his fist he punched the air to emphasize the

Hitler Youth members salute their führer. This impressionable group of ten- to eighteen-year-olds worshiped Hitler as if he were a god.

points he was making. Heck, and thousands of other Hitler Youth, listened to their führer in spellbound silence.

The Secret of Hitler's Success

Nuremberg was not the only city, nor were the young people the only Germans, to be caught in the spell of the charismatic Adolf Hitler. Although one side of his personality was rude, rough, and vulgar, another side was charming, convincing, and believable, and it was this side that brought millions of followers to his feet. Hitler told the German people what they wanted to hear—that conditions in the country would improve, that their own lives would be better, that Germany would become the most powerful nation on earth.

This menacing portrait belies the charming, believable side of Hitler's personality, the side that convinced millions of Germans that he was their messiah.

Hitler, the Roman Emperor

American journalist William Shirer attended the 1934 party rally in Nuremberg, where he got his first introduction to Nazi Germany. He describes the scene in his book Berlin Diary.

"Like a Roman emperor Hitler rode into this medieval town at sundown today past solid [lines] of wildly cheering Nazis who packed the narrow streets. . . . Tens of thousands of Swastika flags blot out the Gothic beauties of the place, the [fronts] of the old houses, the gabled roofs.

For the life of me I could not quite comprehend what hidden springs [Hitler] unloosed in the hysterical mob which was greeting him so wildly. . . . About ten o'clock tonight I got caught in a mob of ten thousand [such] hysterics . . . who jammed the moat in front of Hitler's hotel, shouting: 'We want our *Führer*'. . . . They looked up at him as if he were a Messiah, their faces transformed into something positively inhuman."

His secret, explained one German professor, was "that he wasn't afraid to shout out loud what most Germans were afraid of admitting to themselves, namely that we deserved to rule the world."[5] Even the doubters had to admit that the führer seemed to be bringing good to the country. "You've got to hand it to Hitler," acknowledged one old farmer's wife who took little interest in politics. "He talks big, but he puts everybody to work, even the . . . gypsies."[6]

What was the charm of Adolf Hitler? Was it what he said or how he said it that enthralled his audiences? It was both, explained Otto Strasser, an early follower who worked closely with Hitler but later became one of his harshest critics:

> Adolf Hitler enters a hall. He snuffs the air. For a minute he gropes, feels his way, senses the atmosphere. Suddenly be bursts forth [shouting]:
>
> "The individual has ceased to count. . . . Germany was trampled underfoot. Germans must be united, the interests of each [are not as important as] the interests of all. I will give you back your honour and make Germany invincible. . . ."
>
> His words go like an arrow to their target, he touches each private wound on the raw, . . . expressing [people's] innermost [hopes], telling [them] what [they] most want to hear.[7]

Sometimes a boor, other times an eloquent orator, Adolf Hitler was able to push his way to power by charming some people and bullying others. He began by making speeches at small beer halls in the Bavarian city of Munich. Like his speaking voice, his political career swelled and broke like ocean waves, building to greater heights after each crash. In 1920 Hitler took over a small, poorly financed political group and molded it into his own National Socialist German Workers' Party, the Nazi Party. Just three years later the country claimed fifty thousand card-carrying Nazis. By 1933 the führer had made himself dictator of all Germany, proclaiming that his Third Reich—the third great empire in German history—would last a thousand years.

But 1933 was not the peak of the führer's power. Before he was through, Adolf Hitler held most of Europe under his spell. His vast Third Reich stretched from the Atlantic Ocean into the Soviet

This photo of a 1934 Nuremberg rally shows the enormous strength of the Nazi Party shortly after Hitler had made himself dictator of Germany's Third Reich.

Union, from the Arctic Circle into Africa, and he had embroiled most of the world in war. Millions of people perished during Hitler's reign. Some died fighting for him, others fighting against him, and many more became his innocent victims.

Can Hitler Be Called Great?

While war was raging between armies, navies, and air forces, the führer was waging another—more sinister, evil—war against certain groups of citizens. There was no room in Adolf Hitler's world for anyone who disagreed with him or for those whom he considered inferior. In his passionate pursuit of power, he ordered these undesirables eliminated—wiped from the face of the earth—to make way for himself and his faithful followers. Chief among his victims were the Jews, the Gypsies, and the Jehovah's Witnesses, but Hitler also hated homosexuals, the handicapped, and members of rival political groups like the communists. Millions of these people would suffer torture and death in Nazi-run concentration camps before Hitler's iron grip on the world was broken at last.

Can a person who wreaked such unspeakable horror on mankind really be considered great? Is Hitler's importance to the world the fact that he stands as the ultimate symbol of evil? History remembers people for both positive and negative deeds, explains Professor George Stein:

Hitler regarded himself as a great man. He was not mistaken. Surely it

The starved survivors of a concentration camp in Austria. Hitler ordered the starvation, torture, and death of millions of Jews and other groups that he considered inferior.

would be absurd to suggest that anyone who so [changed] the world was of ordinary stature. The expression "great man," however, implies [something] favorable that most people find impossible to use when referring to the leader of the Third Reich.[8]

In no way, says Stein, did Adolf Hitler leave the German nation, or any other segment of the earth, better off than he found it. His "greatness" was entirely negative and can be measured only by the ruin that he created and the monstrosity of his crimes. Still, there is no doubt that Hitler made an everlasting impression on the world, and for that reason he must be considered important. "If it be conceded that evil can be great, then the quality of greatness cannot . . . be denied him."[9]

1 "In the House of My Parents"

Adolf Hitler,
Mein Kampf

Adolf Hitler, the human tornado that swept across the German countryside, was born on Easter Sunday, April 20, 1889, in the Austrian village of Braunau. Because the town is located on the Inn River, it is called Braunau-am-Inn. Hitler's mother, Klara Pölzl, was a quiet, simple country girl, twenty-three years younger than her husband, Alois Schicklgruber, who had been married twice before. Klara was the nursemaid to Alois's children when she became pregnant by him. A short time later, on January 7, 1885, the two were married. But the child she carried, and two more, died before Adolf was born. Her babies' deaths were very hard on the kind Klara, and perhaps for this reason, she showered Adolf with affection.

Hitler as a baby in Austria. With an overprotective mother and an overbearing father, Hitler's childhood was not a happy one.

The Hitler Family Tree

Alois was not a loving father. He was an illegitimate child, five years old when his mother married his stepfather, J. Georg Hiedler. She died a short time later, and the boy was raised by Johann Nepomuk Hiedler, brother of Georg. When Alois was nearly forty, Johann "took steps to legitimize the young man who had grown up in his house."[10]

He called on the parish priest at Döllersheim and persuaded him to cross out the word "illegitimate" in the register and to [change] a statement signed by three witnesses that his brother . . . Georg Hiedler had accepted the paternity of the child Alois.

Hitler's mother Klara showered him with attention and affection. Although he loved his mother dearly, young Adolf yearned for independence.

This is by no means conclusive evidence, and, in all probability, we shall never know for certain who Adolf Hitler's grandfather . . . really was.[11]

The fact that Hiedler was misspelled Hitler in the register did not seem to bother the men who were changing the birth certificate. But for the rest of the world, that mistake marked a major milestone: one of the most notorious of all last names had now been entered into history. How different events might have been had Alois's birth certificate not been changed, points out writer John Toland: "It is difficult to imagine seventy million Germans shouting in all seriousness, *Heil Schicklgruber!*"[12]

Was Adolf Hitler Part Jewish?

In Nazi Germany, a person with one or two Jewish grandparents was considered a second-rate human being who could be shipped to a slave labor camp or even killed. And yet, say historians John Toland in Adolf Hitler *and Robert Payne in* The Life and Death of Adolf Hitler, *there was some speculation that Hitler himself fit the category.*

"There is the slight possibility that Hitler's grandfather was a wealthy Jew named Frankenberger or Frankenreither; that Maria Anna had [worked] in this Jewish household . . . and the young son had got her pregnant."

"Hans Frank, [later] Governor General of Poland, remembered . . . that toward the end of 1930 he was directed by Hitler to investigate a story that the father of Alois Schicklgruber was the nineteen-year-old son of a Jewish family. . . . He says he found letters written by the Jewish family to Maria Anna Schicklgruber, and that for the first fourteen years of his life regular payments were made for the boy's support. According to Hans Frank the results of his inquiry were 'to the highest degree painful' for Hitler, but he remained unconvinced [that his grandfather was a Jew]. He had heard differently from his father and believed that his grandfather was . . . Georg Hiedler."

The family tree mattered little to young Adolf as he grew up along the German-Austrian border in the last decade of the nineteenth century. Because of Alois's job as a customs official, the Hitler family moved often, living on each side of the river Inn. The time he spent on the German side in the town of Passau, playing with German children, "made a lasting mark on the youngster."[13] It awakened in him a love for Germany that would never die.

His family included his father's children from an earlier marriage—a half brother, Alois Jr., and a half sister, Angela. When Adolf was nearly five, a brother, Edmund, was born, and two years later a sister, Paula. Edmund died before reaching his sixth birthday. Paula lived a quiet, unhappy life; she never married and died sometime in the 1950s.

A Chance to Be Independent

From the day he was born, mother Klara doted on Adolf, and although he loved her, he wanted very much to be independent. At the *Volksschule*, the elementary school that he entered at age six, he found his chance. "All my playing about in the open, the long walk to school [it took more than an hour], and particularly my association with extremely 'husky' boys, which sometimes caused my mother bitter anguish, made me the very opposite of a stay-at-home."[14]

At first Adolf was a good student. His teachers remembered him as alert and noted that he and his sister, Paula, "kept the contents of their school bags in exemplary [ideal] order."[15] During *Volksschule*,

Hitler claims to have had little difficulty with his studies. "School work was ridiculously easy," he bragged in his autobiography, "leaving me so much free time that the sun saw more of me than my room."[16] But this statement, like many others he would make in his life, was filled with exaggeration.

The opposite of Adolf's overprotective mother was his father, Alois. Already past fifty at the time of Adolf's birth, Alois had little patience with the five children who cluttered his home. He began to drink heavily, and during these bouts he became irritable and abusive, often beating his children, his dog, and even his wife. Perhaps because he was the eldest, Alois Jr. of-

Alois Sr. was an abusive alcoholic with little patience for Adolf, who rebelled despite his father's harsh thrashings.

Hitler's Half Brother Looks Back

Long after Adolf's death, his half brother, Alois Jr., remembered him with bitterness. John Toland quotes from a 1948 interview with Alois in his book Adolf Hitler*:*

"He was imperious [arrogant] and quick to anger from childhood onward and would not listen to anyone. My stepmother always took his part. He would get the craziest notions and get away with it. If he didn't have his way he got very angry. . . .

He had no friends, took to no one and could be very heartless. He could fly into a rage over any triviality."

Hitler's older brother Alois Jr. left home at the age of fourteen. Alois later remembered Adolf as an arrogant bully who always insisted on getting his own way.

ten got the worst beatings. But rarely did Klara step in to help him, as she did her own son, Adolf. As a result, Alois grew to resent his half brother.

The older boy's answer was to run away from home at age fourteen, leaving Adolf to bear the brunt of his father's temper. With Alois Jr. gone, Adolf kept "cool but friendly relationships with his sister and half-sister,"[17] but their home life was hardly pleasant. His sister Paula recalled violent encounters between Adolf and their father, especially when Alois tried to impress his son with his importance as a government official. Adolf had a way of angering his father, of arousing him "to extreme harsh-

Hitler (top row, center) in elementary school. Here, the future dictator of Germany first demonstrated his leadership abilities.

ness," and as a result, Paula remembered, the boy "got his sound thrashing every day."[18] The punishments did not seem to frighten him, however, nor cause him to give in to his father's demands.

> He was a scrubby little rogue, and all attempts . . . to thrash him for his rudeness and to cause him to love the profession of an official of the state were in vain. How often on the other hand did my mother caress him and try to obtain with her kindness, where the father could not succeed with harshness![19]

Yet even Klara had little control over her son. At the end of five years, when it was time for Adolf to advance to the next level of school, he had two choices. He could go to the gymnasium, which focused on the arts and prepared students for college, or to the *Realschule*, a more practical, technical school.

A Desire to Become a Painter

In Adolf's mind there was no doubt. He would go to the gymnasium, or secondary school, and study to be an artist. In Alois's mind there was no doubt either. His son would go to the *Realschule* and prepare for a career. In vain Alois tried to inspire the boy with stories of his own success as a customs officer. But Adolf wanted no part of it; his heart was set on becoming a painter.

Alois won the first battle, and in 1900 his son entered the *Realschule* at Linz, a city near the Austrian town where the family had moved a year earlier. Adolf was unhappy here. In the *Volksschule* he had been a leader in his class; at Linz, he was nobody, a country boy looked down on by his city classmates. The school was in "a gloomy four story building on a narrow street. [Cold] and forbidding, it looked more like an office building than a school."[20] Classes were large, and Adolf no longer received the special attention he had gotten from teachers at the *Volksschule*. In his misery he failed the first year.

The second went a little better. Slowly he began to take command of his fellow classmates, just as he had led them at the *Volksschule*. "We all liked him, at desk and at play," said one boy. "He had 'guts.' He wasn't a hothead . . . he was a *quiet fanatic*."[21]

It was fanatically German that Hitler was becoming, even though he was an Austrian citizen. He took great pride in his blue eyes and light brown hair. These, he told his classmates, were the features of true Germanic people—unlike their own brown eyes and dark hair. Later, as he rose to power, Hitler built this image of the blond-haired, blue-eyed German into what he called the pure Aryan race—a superior breed of humankind that he claimed "has been and is the bearer of human cultural development."[22]

As a leader at the school, Hitler showed promise; but as a student, his future held little. The second year's improvement did not last long; soon he began having problems with mathematics, a subject that troubled him throughout his school days. At the same time, there was trouble at home.

Adolf Hitler: Painter? Artist?

Young Adolf's desire to become a painter caused bitter arguments with his father. In Mein Kampf, *Hitler recalls their disagreements.*

"How it happened, I myself do not know, but one day it became clear to me that I would become a painter, an artist. There was no doubt as to my talent for drawing; it had been one of my father's reasons for sending me to the *Realschule*, but never in all the world would it have occurred to him to give me professional training in this direction. On the contrary. When for the first time . . . I was asked what I myself wanted to be, and I rather abruptly blurted out the decision I had made, my father for the moment was struck speechless.

'Painter? Artist?'

'Artist, no, never as long as I live!'

But since his son . . . had apparently inherited his father's stubbornness, the same answer came back at him. Except, of course, that it was in the opposite sense.

And thus the situation remained on both sides. My father did not depart from his 'Never!' And I intensified my 'Oh, yes!'"

Just after the start of the new year, on January 3, 1903, Alois suffered severe internal bleeding and died very suddenly. His father's death meant that thirteen-year-old Adolf was now the male head of the house.

Alois's death must have been a relief to the family in many ways, for no longer would his fits of temper and brutal arguments enflame the household. Yet Adolf later wrote that the event "plung[ed] us all into the depths of grief"[23] and claimed that although his father had been strict, the discipline had never hurt him. Over the years the irritation he had felt toward his father mellowed, and he wrote about him in a positive way, acknowledging the impact he had made on his life:

[My father's greatest] desire had been to help his son forge his career, thus preserving [me] from his own bitter experience [as a boy]. In this, to all appearances, he had not succeeded. But, though unwittingly, he had sown the seed for a future which at that time neither he nor I would have comprehended.[24]

Nor could anyone else in the world have comprehended what future lay in store for this dreamer and drifter. Who could have guessed, as the new century dawned, what evil would sprout from the seeds planted by the now-dead Alois Hitler?

2 "The Most Miserable Time of My Life"

Adolf Hitler, *Mein Kampf*

With his father gone, Adolf was now in control of his own future. He continued to do poorly in school, not because he was stupid but because he was lazy. He resented his teachers for trying to discipline him and they, in turn, showed little concern for him.

The *Völkisch* Movement

One person at the *Realschule*, however—history professor Leopold Pötsch—did make an impact on Adolf Hitler's life. Pötsch was a follower of the growing *völkisch* movement, a group of fanatic Germans who believed in the superiority of the Germanic people. They felt that the *Volk*, "people," were being threatened by foreigners, particularly Jews. The purpose of government, they claimed, was to protect and promote the lives of the *Volk*; everyone else was inferior. "We are the blond race of the north," proclaimed the *völkisch* newspaper. "We are the noble people of the world."[25]

The influence of the *völkisch* movement stayed with Adolf long after his time at the *Realschule* ended. At the close of the 1904 term, when he was fifteen, he was expelled because of failing grades. At the

same time, and with the same lack of enthusiasm, he was going through confirmation classes at the Linz cathedral. His sponsor at the church remembered him clearly, for among the boys being confirmed, "none was so sulky and surly as Adolf Hitler. . . . It was almost as though the whole business, the whole confirmation was repugnant to him."[26]

In the fall Klara arranged for Adolf to enter another *Realschule*, this one at Steyr, a town about twenty-five miles from Linz. The boy was miserable here and spent his days shooting rats from the window of the dingy room where he lived. Nevertheless his grades improved, and he was asked to return the next fall to take examination for entry into the next level, the *Oberrealschule*. The idea of more schooling was repulsive to Adolf, so he put it temporarily out of his mind.

That summer he traveled with his mother to Spital, a small farming area where they visited her sister, Adolf's Aunt Theresia, and her family. Here he became ill with a lung disease that affected his breathing. "Adolf will never be healthy after this sickness,"[27] the doctor told Aunt Theresia. In truth, the disease may actually have been a good excuse to end his studies, for Adolf later wrote, "Suddenly an illness came to my help."[28] So it was that at age sixteen Adolf Hitler's formal education came to an end.

A Passion for Opera

The dropout spent his days dreaming and drawing, filling many sketchbooks with mediocre illustrations of buildings around Linz. Under the constant care of his mother, Adolf often slept until midmorning. At night he stayed up late reading books on art and history, along with the American cowboy and Indian stories of Karl May, a widely popular German author who had never set foot in the United States. Adolf also had a passion for opera and regularly visited the Linz Opera House. Here, in the fall of 1905 he met the one real friend of his teenage years, August Kubizek.

Adolf was quickly drawn to the young man he called Gustl, and Gustl likewise admired him. According to biographer Robert Payne, "Kubizek was impressed by Adolf's strangeness, his pallor, his burning eyes, and his long speeches delivered in a voice of extraordinary urgency about anything that came into his mind." [29] Gustl worked for his father, who ran an upholstery shop, but his dream was to become a musician, and he well understood Adolf's similar dream of becoming an artist. Together the two strolled the streets of Linz, discussing their futures and—when they could afford it—going to operas.

One opera that particularly impressed Hitler was *Rienzi*. The tale was set in Roman times and the music was written by

Hitler was passionate about art and dreamed of making it his career. He painted this picture as an aspiring artist in 1910.

Richard Wagner, a composer Hitler grew to admire above all others. In the story Rienzi is a leader of the common people, whose goal is to free them from the tyranny of wealthy lords. Although he defends the common folk, Rienzi is never really one of them. The citizens treat him like a god or a king, shouting *"Heil, Rienzi!"* when he passes. And although he is a hero, Rienzi seems to know that a tragic end awaits him. In the last act he stands amid the ruins of his burning house shouting, "No more applause greets me, who gave you peace and freedom!"[30]

Immediately after the performance Hitler insisted that he and Gustl climb a nearby mountain, although it was nearly midnight. Once on top, Gustl noted, Adolf became distant and withdrawn, like Rienzi himself, lost in his own dreams. The opera, said Kubizek, seemed to have changed the course of Hitler's life:

> Now he aspired to something higher, something I could not yet fully understand. All this surprised me, because I believed that the [life] of an artist was for him the highest of all goals, the one most worth striving for. But now he was speaking of an [order] he would one day receive from the people, to lead them out of [slavery] to the heights of freedom.[31]

Many years later, after Hitler had become Germany's führer, he was reminded of the first time he had seen *Rienzi*. "In that hour it began,"[32] he said soberly, speaking of his inspiration to lead the German *Volk*.

Along with opera, art and architecture became a passion with Adolf. He and Kubizek spent countless days walking the streets of Linz, admiring its structures and planning how they would change the design or location of certain buildings. Adolf made sketches of his favorites and planned in detail a house where he and Kubizek would live together, spending their lives surrounded by art, music, and beauty.

Love and Sorrow

His friendship with Kubizek did not mean that women never entered Adolf's mind. It was in Linz that he first fell in love, with a girl he and Gustl met on their walks around town. Her name was Stefanie Jansten, and although he never spoke to her, Adolf remained madly in love with her for nearly three years. Their only communication was a smile or a nod of the head as they passed on the street. Still, he was convinced that Stefanie knew what he was thinking, that she understood his hopes and dreams. In vain, Kubizek tried to bring his friend back to reality:

> When I suggested that it was quite possible that she was not in the least concerned about his ideas because he had never spoken to Stefanie about them, he became furious and screamed at me: "You understand nothing! You have not the slightest comprehension of an extraordinary love!"
>
> To quiet him, I asked him whether it was possible for him to communicate complicated ideas to Stefanie by exchanging long glances with her. He only said, "It is possible. No one can explain these things. All that is in me is also in Stefanie!"[33]

Apparently Stefanie did not share, or even realize, the depth of Adolf's love for

Richard Wagner's Influence on Hitler

"Whoever wants to understand National Socialist Germany must know Wagner," Hitler used to say of German musician Richard Wagner. In *his book* The Rise and Fall of the Third Reich, *journalist William Shirer explains Wagner's influence on Hitler.*

"From his earliest days Hitler worshiped Wagner. . . . It was . . . his towering operas [with] German . . . heroic myths, . . . fighting pagan gods and heroes, . . . demons and dragons, . . . blood feuds and primitive tribal codes, . . . the splendor of love and life and nobility of death, which inspired the myths of modern Germany . . . which Hitler and the Nazis . . . took over as their own.

. . . Though Richard Wagner harbored a fanatical hatred, as Hitler did, for the Jews, who he was convinced were out to dominate the world with their money, and though he scorned . . . democracy . . . and the materialism and mediocrity of the [middle class], he also fervently hoped that the Germans, 'with their special gifts,' would 'become not rulers, but [nobles] of the world.'"

German composer Richard Wagner, whose grand opera Reinzi *had a lasting impact on young Hitler.*

her. When Kubizek suggested that he introduce himself, Adolf refused, worried that she would ask what he did for a living, and he would have to admit that he had no career.

Perhaps to answer that question, and perhaps because it was time for him to pursue his dream, Adolf decided to go to Vienna, the capital city of Austria, to attend operas and get serious about his art. Being accepted to the General Painting School of the Vienna Academy of Fine Arts was his goal. In the fall of 1907, when he was eighteen, he took the entrance examination. Although his drawings were passable, they were not good enough to gain him admission.

Bitter and disappointed, he returned home to Linz to face even greater depression. His beloved mother Klara, who suffered from breast cancer, was in failing health, and Adolf decided to stay in Linz to care for her. Unfortunately Klara was beyond his help, or even that of Dr. Bloch, the Jewish family physician. On December 21, despite their best efforts, Klara died. "In all my career," said Bloch, who was a friend of the family, "I never saw anyone so prostrate [overcome] with grief as Adolf Hitler."[34]

Shortly after his mother's funeral Hitler returned to Vienna, and in a short time Kubizek arrived to study music. The two lived together in a dismal, bug-ridden room, until Gustl was drafted into the army. Still desperate to become an artist, Hitler decided to take lessons, in the hope of passing the academy's examinations on

Hitler was grief-stricken over his mother's death in 1907. She was buried alongside her husband at this site in Linz, Austria. German soldiers pay their respects to the grave in 1938.

his second try. It was useless; the examiner made the good suggestion that he study architecture instead, since his drawings were more technical than artistic. But this would have meant returning to a *Realschule*, which Hitler did not want to do.

A Future Bleak and Black

Angry and depressed, he moved into a new, equally dingy room, cutting off all correspondence with his family and Kubizek. The city of Vienna, which Hitler had once believed to be the center of beauty and culture, now looked bleak and black to him. He fit in with no one and began to hate those around him. Although his parents had left him some money, it soon ran low. Finally, in desperation, he entered an asylum for the homeless, just before Christmas 1909.

For a person who dreamed of being a leader of men and considered himself in a class above common laborers, living in a homeless shelter was a bitter blow. As he sat on his cot, alone and dejected, another resident approached him. Reinhold Hanisch, a tramp who was also an aspiring artist, offered to show Hitler the ropes of poverty living—how to survive the winter

"A World of Misery and Poverty"

In Mein Kampf *Hitler describes his days in Vienna. Although the language he uses is flowery, the depth of his misery can still be seen.*

"To me Vienna, the city which, to so many . . . is a festive playground for merrymakers, represents, I am sorry to say, merely the living memory of the saddest period of my life. . . . Five years in which I was forced to earn a living, first as a day laborer, then as a small painter . . . hunger was then my faithful bodyguard; he never left me for a moment and partook of all I had. . . .

In this period my eyes were opened to two menaces of which I had previously scarcely known the names, and whose terrible importance for the existence of the German people I certainly did not understand: Marxism and Jewry. . . .

I owe it to that period that I grew hard and am still capable of being hard. And even more, I [praise] it for tearing me away from the hollowness of comfortable life . . . for hurling me, despite all resistance, into a world of misery and poverty, thus making me acquainted with those for whom I was later to fight."

in ragged clothes, how to beg on the streets of Vienna. To Hanisch it was unbelievable how a young man who seemed as talented and intelligent as Hitler could end up in a place like the homeless asylum. When he questioned his friend, Adolf simply replied, "I don't know myself."[35] Hitler, Hanisch concluded, was lazy and moody:

> Over and over again, there were days on which he simply refused to work. Then he would hang around night shelters, living on the bread and soup that he got there, and discussing politics, often getting involved in heated controversies.[36]

Hitler spent his years in Vienna reading, painting, and forming ideas about the way the world should be. His fanatic nationalism—belief in the superiority of the German homeland—led him to read and study the *völkisch* movement in greater

Hitler lived for five years in the anti-Semitic Austrian capital of Vienna (left). Here, he spent his time learning about the anti-Semitic, fanatically German völkisch *movement, and painting the buildings around the city. Pictured above is one of Hitler's works painted while he was in Vienna..*

detail. From his reading he formed the basis for what would one day become the National Sozialistische Deutsche Arbeiter Partei, the National Socialist German Workers' Party.

After some time he moved from the homeless asylum to a higher class men's home called the Männerheim, where he was soon joined by Hanisch. The two formed a business partnership; Adolf painted postcards or pictures for frame makers to display in their frames, and Hanisch was the salesman. In theory they shared the profits, but after a few months Hitler became suspicious and had Hanisch arrested for taking more than his share.

The failed artist was becoming increasingly consumed by politics. He spent long hours reading newspapers and history books and preaching his ideas to anyone who would listen. He showed little interest in working, in women, or in settling down to a normal life. On those occasions when he did make a little money, he spent it quickly, rarely saving for his next time of need. People considered him strange and eccentric.

A Burning in His Soul

Unlike many of those with whom he associated, Hitler did not smoke or drink. He was driven by a passion for politics and public speaking that seemed to burn in his soul. It burned even stronger, Hanisch recalled, after Hitler saw a movie titled *Tunnel*. In it, a rebel rallies masses of people through the power of his fiery speeches. "Hitler almost went crazy," Hanisch recalled. "The impression it

---

Struggle Is the Father of All Things

Hitler's belief in the victory of the strongest—who, in his mind, were the German nation and the German people— was made clear in three of his early speeches, quoted in Gordon Prange's book, Hitler's Words.

"The idea of struggle is as old as life itself. . . . In this struggle, the stronger, the more able win, while the less able, the weak lose."

"As it is with the individual so it is in . . . nations. Only by struggle are the strong able to raise themselves above the weak. . . . For if you do not fight for life, then life will never be won."

"Whatever goal man has reached is due to his [wits] plus his brutality. . . . There will never be a solution to the German problem until we return to the three . . . principles which control the [life] of every nation: The concept of struggle, the purity of blood, and the [cleverness] of the individual."

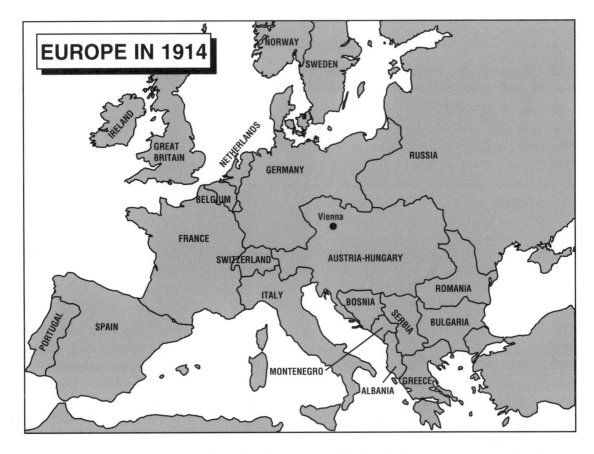

EUROPE IN 1914

made on him was so strong that for days afterwards he spoke of nothing except the power of the spoken word."[37]

At the Männerheim, he became close friends with two Jewish men. In fact, although most people in Vienna at that time were fierce anti-Semites who hated Jews, Hitler's acquaintances do not recall that he ever spoke in anger against a Jew. Indeed, he called one "a very decent man" and told Hanisch that he preferred Jewish businessmen "because only they were willing to take chances."[38] Hitler even claimed to be a bit shocked by the anti-Semitism shown in the newspapers of Vienna, saying

this kind of writing was "unworthy of . . . a great nation."[39]

But after more than five years in anti-Semitic Vienna, a city under the leadership of a Jew-hating mayor, Hitler's own prejudices did take root. Here he had faced poverty, humiliation, and rejection in most of his goals, and these bitter experiences were the seed of what would one day become his own violent anti-Semitism. He blamed his failure on the Jews, calling them "cod-hearted, shameless, and calculating."[40] It was in this frame of mind that he decided to put Vienna behind him and leave the cultured city he had grown to hate.

3 "An Exceptionally Brave, Effective, and Conscientious Soldier"

in Charles Bracelen Flood,
Hitler: The Path to Power

Leaving behind the misery and disappointment of Vienna, Adolf Hitler set out in May 1913 for Munich, capital of the mountainous state of Bavaria. At that time Bavaria was independent but held close ties to the German empire. From the moment he arrived, Hitler was overcome by a "heartfelt love which seized me for this city more than for any other place that I knew." His dream was "to make a name for myself as an architect and . . . to dedicate my sincere services to the nation."[41]

Reporting for Military Duty

But some people claimed there was another reason why Hitler had left Austria: to avoid serving in the military. Since 1909 he had been old enough for military service but had never registered; now the police were looking for him. They found him in Munich in January 1914 and ordered him to return to Linz, Austria. Protesting that he did not have the money or time to travel so far, he wrote a letter, asking permission to report for duty instead at Salzburg, an Austrian city much closer to Munich. His long letter shows some of the diplomatic charm for which Hitler would one day be famous. In it he explains why he had failed to register for military service in 1909:

> I can only plead that I had fallen on very bad times. I was an inexperienced young man without any financial resources and much too proud to accept help from strangers, let alone ask for it. . . . For two years my only companions were sorrow, poverty and constant hunger. I have never learned the meaning of the beautiful word "youth", and even today, five years later, I still carry the memory of those days in the form of frostbites on my fingers and toes. . . . Despite cruel poverty in what were often dubious surroundings, I have always kept my name decent and completely spotless before the law and before my own conscience.[42]

He ended the letter by claiming that reporting for military service was "a duty of which I was not aware at the time" and begged the authorities "not to make things unnecessarily difficult for me."[43] Amazingly, his wishes were granted. He was allowed to report at Salzburg, which he did on February 5. There it was decided that Adolf Hitler was "unfit for combatant and auxiliary duties, too weak. Unable to bear arms."[44]

But events that soon would escalate into World War I changed Hitler's mind about military service. On June 28, 1914, Archduke Francis Ferdinand, heir to the Austrian throne, was shot and killed by a young Serbian nationalist. Across Europe rumors of war spread wildly. Germany and Bavaria promised to help Austria; Russia pledged its support to the Serbs. Soon other countries were drawn into the fray. In the streets of Munich, thousands of people rallied for war, among them Adolf Hitler.

Like millions of other young men, Hitler was eager to enlist. Here was the chance to help thrust Germany into a position of power on the world stage. It was also a chance to overcome the personal frustration and disappointment that had haunted Hitler for years. "For me, as for every other German, the most memorable period of my life now began."[45]

The Cold Reality of War

Two days after war was declared on August 1, 1914, Hitler wrote a letter to Ludwig III, king of Bavaria, asking to join the Bavarian army. Permission granted, he began training, and just sixty-five days later was crouching in the front lines of battle. From the front Adolf sent letters to his landlady, Anna Popp, who owned the house where he had lived in Munich. On October 20 he wrote about spending one rainy night in a stable, where "I was wet through. . . . On Sunday we were on the move again from 5 A.M. to 6 P.M., all of us dog-tired, fighting action after action."[46] Still, Hitler

Hitler (front row, far left) with his World War I regiment. Eager to help his beloved Germany become a world power, Hitler fought valiantly and received military awards for bravery.

was extremely proud of himself and his regiment, as he told Anna Popp's husband in a letter dated December 4, soon after he received the Iron Cross Second Class, a military award for bravery:

For 4 days we were engaged in the fiercest battle, and I can proudly say that our regiment fought like heroes. On the very first day, we lost nearly all our officers. . . . I have, so to speak, been risking my life every day, looking death straight in the eye. . . .

On 2 December, I finally received the Iron Cross. It was the happiest day of my life. True, most of my comrades who had earned it just as much were dead. I beg you, dear Herr Popp, please save the newspaper in which the decoration is listed. I would like to have it as a keepsake if the Lord should spare my life.[47]

Under Divine Protection

During World War I Hitler believed God protected him in battle because he was destined one day to rule the world. Walter C. Langer, in his book The Mind of Adolf Hitler, *quotes one of Hitler's many "proofs" of this theory.*

"I was eating my dinner in a trench with several comrades. Suddenly a voice seemed to be saying to me, 'Get up and go over there.' It was so clear and insistent that I obeyed automatically, as if it had been a military order. I rose at once to my feet and walked twenty yards along the trench carrying my dinner in its tin can with me.

Then I sat down to go on eating, my mind being once more at rest. Hardly had I done so when a flash and deafening report came from the part of the trench I had just left. A stray shell had burst over the group in which I had been sitting, and every member of it was killed."

For four long years fighting raged throughout central Europe. It was particularly heavy in France, where soldiers fought from trenches dug across the beautiful French countryside. Millions of men were killed and grotesquely injured, without either side coming close to victory. Throughout the fighting the Popps continued to receive letters and postcards from Adolf, telling them about conditions at the front. "This endless battle dulls one's senses," he wrote. "Above all we lack regular sleep." On January 26, 1915, he reported that the constant fighting had claimed a great many victims, but "I myself am miraculously well."[48] His comrades had noticed that, too. Said one of them to him after a day of particularly heavy fighting, "For you, there is no bullet!"[49] Adolf simply grinned.

As the reality of war became more horrible and more personal, many of the men prayed that they would be wounded—not enough to do permanent injury, but severely enough to take them out of battle and home to their families. Not so with Hitler, whose family meant little to him. In October 1916, in the midst of fierce fighting at the Somme River in France, he was hit by a shell fragment in his upper left leg. As he lay on a stretcher on the battlefield, he pleaded with his commander, "It isn't so bad, Lieutenant, right? I can still stay with you, I mean, stay with the regiment! Can't I?"[50] The battlefield trenches were his home; this is where he wanted to be. Although Hitler spent nearly five months in a hospital near Berlin recovering from his wounds, he eventually returned to the front.

By April 1917 soldiers on both sides were exhausted. It was then that the United States entered the war against Germany. For more than a year troops on both sides fought fiercely, and throughout it all there was no soldier braver than Adolf Hitler. On August 4, 1918, he was awarded the highly prized Iron Cross First Class, "for personal bravery and general merit."[51]

By now, however, the Austro-German forces were beginning to weaken. New methods of warfare were being tried on the battlefield, and one of them—poisonous mustard gas—was especially fright-

ful. On the night of October 13 Hitler came face to face with it. His unit was fighting on a hill in Belgium, where poisonous gas shells exploded all around:

> [About midnight] a number of us passed out, a few of our comrades forever. Toward morning I, too, was seized with pain which grew worse with every quarter hour, and at seven in the morning I stumbled and tottered back with burning eyes. . . . A few hours later, my eyes had turned into glowing coals; it had grown dark around me.[52]

War's Bitter Aftermath

Hitler was taken to a nearby hospital, where he lay for days not knowing if he would see again. As he listened to the talk around him, he began to sense "some-

(Right) French soldiers attack German trenches with gas and flames. Hitler was almost blinded by such an attack while fighting in Belgium. In addition he received a shell fragment wound. In spite of the everyday horrors of war, Hitler felt at home in the battlefield trenches (above).

thing indefinite but repulsive in the air."[53] Slowly piecing together snatches of conversation, he realized with horror that Germany had lost the war. His beloved fatherland was about to surrender. On November 10 a pastor came to the hospital to confirm the terrible news: Deutschland—Germany—lay in defeat. Adolf Hitler was in despair, his comrades dead, his own dreams shattered.

The agreement that officially ended World War I was the Treaty of Versailles, named for the French city in which it was signed in June 1919. The treaty put nearly impossible demands and restrictions on the German people, for world leaders were determined to see that the country never again became powerful. Large amounts of land that had belonged to Germany before the war were now divided among France, Belgium, and Poland. The victors demanded that Germany assume all guilt for starting the war and pay the costs of all damage done to civilians during the years of fighting. France insisted on occupying the Rhineland, a section of southwestern Germany, for the next fifteen years. Germany was ordered not to rebuild its military forces or equipment.

The German people, along with several world leaders, thought the treaty was much too harsh. Said American president Woodrow Wilson, "If I were a German, I think I should never sign it."[54] Future president Herbert Hoover predicted it would "pull down all Europe and so injure the United States."[55]

But under widespread pressure to make peace, German leaders did sign the treaty, not knowing how their people would bear the heavy burdens that were about to be thrust on them. Adolf Hitler

POST-WORLD WAR I
EUROPE

This map shows Europe about 1923, after the Treaty of Versailles had taken effect. Many central and eastern European nations won their independence from what had been Germany, Russia, and Austria-Hungary.

Duty and Heroism

In Mein Kampf, *Hitler wrote about a personal battle that nearly every soldier fought—the struggle between fear and duty. His words leave no doubt about his supreme love for Germany and the fierce pride he felt for his adopted country.*

"The romance of battle had been replaced by horror. The enthusiasm gradually cooled and the . . . joy was stifled by mortal fear. The time came when every man had to struggle between the instinct of self-preservation and . . . duty [to one's country]. After a long inner struggle . . . duty emerged victorious . . . . The young volunteer had become an old soldier. . . .

Thousands of years may pass, but never will it be possible to speak of heroism without mentioning the German army and the World War. Then from the veil of the past the iron front of the gray steel helmet will emerge, unwavering and unflinching. . . . As long as there are Germans alive, they will remember that these men were sons of their nation."

followed the events from Munich, where he had returned after leaving the army hospital, his eyesight still not fully restored. During those days of recovery, Hitler's vision of his own future and that of his beloved Germany began to be clear. "I, for my part," he wrote, "decided to go into politics."[56]

Reshaping the German Workers' Party

It was a good time to enter German politics, for the country was in a state of tremendous upheaval and revolution. People were discontented; they were looking for leadership. Many political groups sprang up, each with its own idea of how the country should be run. Hitler, still attached to the military, was ordered to take a course in political instruction. At the end of the course, one of his assignments was to learn more about a small political group, the Deutsche Arbeiter Partei (DAP), or German Workers' Party. The party had been formed about a year earlier by Anton Drexler, a locksmith from Munich. Its aim was to attract working-class people who held a strong belief in the superiority of the German nation. Hitler agreed with some of the party's ideas, but he was not impressed with its size or leadership. "This was the life of a little club at the lowest possible level. Was I to join an organization like this?"[57]

Nevertheless, Hitler was drawn to the party, for he saw that he might transform it to suit his own goals. After attending a few meetings, he began working to make the party bigger and better known by

Had It All Been in Vain?

After hearing the news of Germany's surrender in World War I, Adolf Hitler was overcome with tears, grief, and feelings of despair. In Mein Kampf, *he describes how he lost all hope and began looking for someone to blame.*

"I tottered and groped my way back to the dormitory, threw myself on my bunk, and dug my burning head into my blanket and pillow.

Since the day when I had stood at my mother's grave, I had not wept. . . . But now I could not help it. Only now did I see how all personal suffering vanishes in comparison with the misfortune of the fatherland.

And so it had all been in vain. . . . Was it for this that the German soldier had stood fast in the sun's heat and in snowstorms, hungry, thirsty, and freezing, weary from sleepless nights and endless marches?

The more I tried to [understand] the monstrous event in this hour, the more the shame of indignation and disgrace burned my brow. . . .There followed terrible days and even worse nights—I knew that all was lost. . . . In these nights hatred grew in me, hatred for those responsible for this deed."

arranging for a larger meeting hall, advertising in the paper, and convincing organizers to let him speak. His first speech, at Munich's Hofbräuhaus Keller in October 1919, was attended by 111 people. Although he was not then an effective speaker, Hitler pledged himself to shape the party into a major political force and vowed to let nothing stand in his way.

About the same time, the army began looking at Hitler as "an authority on the Jewish problem." In his first real political document—a letter to an army agent—he outlined "the proper attitude to be cultivated toward the Jews." In it, he accused the Jews of profiting from the upheaval in Germany and of being the "driving forces of the revolution" that was then sweeping the country. He ended his letter by suggesting that "the final aim [of government] must be the deliberate removal of the Jews."[58]

The tool that Hitler needed to achieve his political goals was handed to him on January 1, 1920. This was a card that officially made him the fifty-fifth general member and seventh committee member of the DAP. In less than a decade Hitler would transform this tiny party into a major force in German politics.

4 "I Alone Bear the Responsibility"

Adolf Hitler in Alan Bullock,
Hitler: A Study in Tyranny

Even before Adolf Hitler became an official member of the DAP, he started work on a party program. The party needed a purpose, a focus, a set of goals. How did the group feel about important political issues? What beliefs did the party support? And, of course, what was its policy on Jews?

The Twenty-Five-Point Program

To clarify these questions, Hitler drew up a twenty-five-point program to present at a meeting in a Munich *Hofbräuhaus* ("beer hall") on February 24, 1920. His early worries that the meeting might be poorly attended were swept away when he entered the hall to find nearly two thousand people. Within the crowd he expected detractors, or belittlers, and troublemakers, but he was prepared. Friends in the army had promised to arrange protection and stop any violent protests that might erupt.

In the audience were common, working people—the folks suffering most under Germany's new government, the Weimar Republic. Hitler talked to them about the government's failure to provide jobs, about the lack of health care, and dozens of other issues. He spoke about

the threat of inflation, warning that German money was on its way to becoming worthless. Hitler accused the Jews of benefiting from these hard times and promised that the DAP would not put up with Jewish greed and lust for money. There is only one way, said Hitler, to bring about "a

Hitler gained the support of the German working class by using the Jews as scapegoats for the country's suffering.

lasting recovery of our *Volk*," and that is to support the idea of "Common good before individual good."[59] The welfare of the masses, he preached, was more important than the success of a few people.

Carrying his condemnation of Jews one step further, Hitler claimed that only people with so-called pure German blood could become citizens. "Hence no Jew can be a countryman,"[60] he concluded; nor could they hold public office. As a solution he suggested deporting all Jews who had entered the country after the start of World War I. If necessary to improve the lives of Aryan Germans, all Jews would be expelled.

Most of Hitler's twenty-five points began with the words "We demand." The party demanded that the hateful Treaty of Versailles be "abrogated," or nullified. The party demanded that the government take steps to "ensure that every citizen shall have the possibility of living decently and earning a livelihood."[61] The party demanded the formation of a people's army to replace the regular army. The party demanded strict rules on the language and content of German newspapers. As he explained his points, Hitler stopped after each one to see if his listeners understood and agreed with it.

Rabble-rousers in the audience were quickly put down by Hitler's army troopers who were "swift as greyhounds, tough as leather, and hard as . . . steel."[62] His speech had tremendous impact. Nearly everyone in the audience found some of the twenty-five points to their liking. Hitler "made things understandable even to the foggiest brain," reported Hans Frank, a lawyer in the audience who would later become one of the highest ranking Nazis. He got "to the core of things."[63]

The NSDAP Is Born

No longer was there any question about Hitler's ability to influence his audience. Those in the party who did not agree with him were soon silenced. Within a few months Hitler had changed the name of the party to the National Sozialistische Deutsche Arbeiter Partei (NSDAP), or National Socialist German Workers' Party, and adopted the swastika as the party's official symbol. He also designed the flag—a field of red with a white circle in the center. The black swastika inside the circle represented the German people's struggle "for the victory of Aryan man . . . which is eternally anti-Semitic and always will be anti-Semitic."[64]

German troops proudly carry the NSDAP flag bearing the party's official symbol—the swastika. The swastika symbolized the German people's struggle "for the victory of Aryan man."

Psychoanalyzing Adolf Hitler

Psychoanalyst Walter C. Langer decided that Hitler identified with the victors in World War I so strongly that he put himself in their place and made the Jews his enemies. This excerpt is from Langer's book The Mind of Adolf Hitler.

"He is now practicing on the Jews . . . the things he feared the victors might do to him. . . . First, it [gives] him the opportunity of appearing before the world as the . . . brute he imagines himself to be; second, it [gives] him the opportunity of proving to himself that he is as heartless and brutal as he wants to be . . . ; third, in eliminating the Jews he unconsciously feels that he is ridding himself, and Germany, of the poison that is responsible for all difficulties; fourth, as the masochist [one who enjoys hurting himself] he really is, he derives . . . pleasure from the suffering of others in whom he can see himself; fifth, he can [release] his bitter hatred and contempt of the world in general by using the Jew as a scapegoat."

Steadily Hitler's power increased. Thanks to the help of Ernst Röhm, an army captain who had joined the party before Hitler, the group was able to buy the *Völkischer Beobachter*, a weekly newspaper that soon became a daily. Röhm was important to Hitler in another way. Believing that the key to a strong government was getting the army involved in politics, he gathered some of the toughest former soldiers he could find and ordered them to protect party speakers at public gatherings. This group of storm troopers later became known as the Sturmabteilung (SA), or Brownshirts, named for the color of their uniforms.

Not only did the Brownshirts protect, they also stirred up trouble when there was none happening. Hitler believed that a show of power was an important part of propaganda—the advertising he did constantly to strengthen the image of the NSDAP. He welcomed hecklers and troublemakers at party gatherings, and when they did not appear, some of his allies in the audience created a chaotic scene that would give the Brownshirts a chance to show their strength.

The NSDAP was becoming the stage from which Adolf Hitler would launch his political career. In the summer of 1921 he traveled to Berlin, the German capital, to speak to organizations whose political ideas seemed similar to his own. While he was gone, Anton Drexler and other original members of the DAP met to protest the direction in which they saw the party heading. What they decided to do was print flyers to distribute among members. The flyers read:

A lust for power and personal ambition have caused Herr Adolf Hitler to return to his post after six weeks'

A group of loyal NSDAP Brownshirts and party members listen intently to their leader. Hitler was appointed president of the party and given unlimited power after threatening to resign.

absence in Berlin. . . . He regards the time as ripe for bringing dissension and [division] into our ranks by means of shadowy people behind him. . . . It grows more and more clear that his purpose is simply to use the National Socialist Party as a springboard for his own immoral purposes and to seize the leadership in order to force the Party in to a different track at the [right] moment.[65]

Hitler was outraged. He sued Drexler and other party members who had distributed the flyers. Then, using one of his best propaganda tools, he threatened to resign if he were not made president of the party and given unlimited power. No one was surprised when both of those demands were granted. Drexler was at first opposed, but after eight days he was finally persuaded and managed to convince other members of the executive committee of the NSDAP. Drexler, the party's founder, was given the token title of honorary president—a position of no importance or influence.

Armed with his new power, Adolf Hitler set out to become a leading force in German politics, although he was barely known outside Bavaria. He saw himself as the savior of a country that he believed was caving in to the poor leadership of the Weimar Republic and the greed of Jewish businessmen. Every month he drew larger audiences to his speeches in the beer halls of Munich. The power of his voice and message had become contagious; with every public appearance he charmed masses of people:

> For us this man was a whirling dervish. But he knew how to fire up the people, not with arguments, which are never possible in hate speeches, but with the fanaticism of his whole manner, screaming and yelling, and above all by his deafening repetition, and a certain contagious rhythm. This he has learned to do and it has a fearfully exciting primitive and barbaric effect.[66]

The Beer Hall Putsch

As Hitler's popularity grew, so did membership in the NSDAP. By 1923 there were

"He Had the Look of a Fanatic"

Kurt G. W. Ludecke, who later became a faithful follower of National Socialism, was first swept up in Hitler's spell after hearing him speak at a rally in Bavaria in 1922. He remembered that evening in his book I Knew Hitler.

"I was close enough to see Hitler's face, watch every change in his expression, hear every word he said. . . . Critically I studied this slight, pale man, his brown hair parted on one side and falling again and again over his sweating brow. Threatening and [begging], with small, pleading hands and flaming, steel-blue eyes, he had the look of a fanatic.

He urged the revival of German honor and manhood with a blast of words that seemed to cleanse. 'Bavaria is now the most German land in Germany!' he shouted, to roaring applause. . . . Then two last words that were like the sting of a lash: *'Deutschland Erwache!'* 'Awake, Germany!' There was thunderous applause.

I do not know how to describe the emotions that swept over me as I heard this man. His words were like a [whip]. When he spoke of the disgrace of Germany, I felt ready to spring on any enemy. His appeal to German manhood was like a call to arms, the gospel he preached a sacred truth. . . . I forgot everything but the man; then, glancing round, I saw that his magnetism was holding these thousands [of people] as one."

Hitler could mesmerize huge audiences with his convincing, fanatical speaking style.

nearly fifty thousand card-carrying Nazis. But at the same time, Germany was growing weaker because of the poor leadership of the Weimar Republic. The time was right, Hitler could see, for a revolution that would overthrow this helpless government and put someone in power who could restore national pride and German strength. Not surprisingly, he saw that someone as himself.

Gathering around him the most faithful of his followers, Hitler began talking of a coup—a takeover of the Bavarian government. One of the key players in his

The Man Who Was Born to Be a Dictator

Journalist William Shirer writes in his book The Rise and Fall of the Third Reich *that near the end of his trial Hitler "turned his burning eyes directly on the judges," and spoke these words:*

"The man who is born to be a dictator is not [forced to do it]. He wills it. He is not driven forward, but drives himself. . . . The man who feels called upon to govern a people has no right to say, 'If you want me or summon me, I will co-operate.' No! It is his duty to step forward.

For it is not you, gentlemen, who pass judgment on us[the Nazi leaders of the coup]. That judgment is spoken by the eternal court of history. . . . That court will judge us . . . as Germans who wanted only the good of their own people and Fatherland, who wanted to fight and die. You may pronounce us guilty a thousand times over, but the goddess of the eternal court of history will smile and tear to tatters the . . . sentence of this court. For she [finds] us [not guilty]."

This photo of the audience at an early Nazi speech testifies to the popularity of Hitler and the NSDAP, which by 1923 boasted nearly fifty thousand members.

plan was the World War I fighter pilot and hero, Hermann Göring, now in command of the SA. Another war hero, General Erich Ludendorff, also played a major role.

After a few hasty planning sessions, the rebels were ready. On the cold, windy night of November 8, a patriotic meeting was scheduled to take place at the Bürgerbräu Keller, one of Munich's beer halls. As Gustav Kahr, a leader in the Bavarian government, took the stage to speak, Adolf Hitler charged into the hall, pistol in hand, surrounded by a large group of SA men. To the amazement of the crowd, he jumped onto a table, fired a shot into the ceiling, and cried out, "The National Revolution has begun. This hall is occupied by six hundred heavily armed men. No one may leave." He then announced that he had formed a new government with

On trial for their part in the 1923 Beer Hall Putsch, General Ludendorff (far left) and Hitler (second from left) await the verdict of the court. Hitler was sentenced to five years in prison but served only nine months.

General Ludendorff, which was a bold lie. "If I am not victorious by tomorrow afternoon," he proclaimed to the stunned crowd, "I shall be a dead man."[67]

Neither event happened. All night uprisings and street fighting went on. About noon the next day Nazi leaders and two thousand of their followers marched into the center of Munich. Police, who had barricaded the street, opened fire. Sixteen party members and three policemen were killed; Ludendorff was arrested. Caught in the gunfire was Göring, who was cared for by the Jewish owner of a nearby bank. Hitler was also wounded but escaped by car to the home of a wealthy friend and party supporter, where he hid for two days until he was arrested. According to psychoanalyst and author Walter C. Langer in his book *The Mind of Adolf Hitler:*

> It would appear that [Hitler] turned coward on this occasion and that he . . . crawl[ed] away from the scene of the activities. Although he had . . . considerable power and had reason to have some faith in [himself], it seems unlikely that it was [enough] for him to actually engage . . . in physical combat. [He] had temporarily

failed. He went into deep depression and was restrained from committing suicide only by constant reassurances.[68]

With many Nazi leaders now in jail, and their political party prohibited throughout Germany, it seemed that the NSDAP must surely be dead. Adolf Hitler's trial was set for February 26, 1924, but far from seeing his party or his political career as finished, Hitler saw instead a grand opportunity for publicity. He planned just what he would say at his trial and how he would say it. Never would he deny what he had done; he would admit proudly that he and his men had intended—even planned—to overthrow the government.

Hitler spoke eloquently throughout his trial. "I feel myself the best of Germans who wanted the best for the German people,"[69] he told the court. Three of the judges were very impressed by his statements. His part in the Beer Hall Putsch, or uprising, was equal to high treason—disloyalty to one's country. The punishment for his crime was five years in the Landsberg, Bavaria, prison. Part of that time in prison Adolf Hitler would spend creating the blueprint for his destruction of Europe.

5 The NSDAP Is Reborn

The good appearance that Hitler made on the judges and the court apparently gained him special treatment in prison. Throughout his term he "wore his own clothes, was provided with his own rooms and diet, and allowed free association with the 40 other Nazis in jail with him."[70] Unlike most prisoners, he could keep his light on until midnight and could have as many visitors as he liked, provided the visits were supervised.

The Writing of *Mein Kampf*

Even before he entered Landsberg Prison, Adolf Hitler had wanted to write. His plan was to publish a small pamphlet in which he would settle some arguments he was having with certain followers. He wanted to portray himself as the only founder of National Socialism, eliminating Drexler, Röhm, and other early leaders from his history of the party. He also hoped to show the world, through his writing, that Adolf Hitler was not just a superb speaker but a great thinker as well.

That small pamphlet eventually emerged as the first of the two-volume *Mein Kampf.* Rudolf Hess, who later played a key role in the Third Reich and had participated in the Beer Hall Putsch, was imprisoned in Landsberg at the same time as Hitler. During their imprisonment Hitler dictated the book to him. But Hess was no

Hitler (far left) on his thirty-fifth birthday in Landsberg Prison. While incarcerated, Hitler dictated the first of the two-volume Mein Kampf *to fellow prisoner and Beer Hall Putsch participant Rudolf Hess (second from right).*

Mein Kampf: A Program of Blood and Terror

Konrad Heiden, an anti-Nazi writer and historian who fled Germany for the United States, wrote the introduction to the 1971 edition of Mein Kampf. *Tragically, says Heiden, people failed to heed the warnings that Hitler made clear in this book.*

"For years *Mein Kampf* stood as proof of the blindness . . . of the world. For in its pages Hitler announced—long before he came to power—a program of blood and terror [with] such overwhelming frankness that few among its readers had the courage to believe it.

. . . Max Amann, Hitler's business manager . . . hoped that the book would become a source of [money for the party]. Two or three years before Hitler came to power, the sales . . . began to rise, and later they rose astronomically. Amann went on printing the book from the same poor type, on the same cheap paper as before. Everybody was forced to buy it. It was presented as a gift [from the government] to newly-wed couples, but the [marriage] license fee was doubled. *Mein Kampf* made Hitler rich. It became a best-seller second only to the Bible."

great writer, and Hitler was not the great thinker that he wanted the world to believe. Although the book eventually made him much money, *Mein Kampf* is tiresome, tedious reading—often disorganized, inaccurate, and poorly written.

Hitler's release came a little less than nine months into the five-year sentence he was supposed to serve. "Behind the scenes," says historian Charles Bracelen Flood, "the three . . . judges who had been so impressed by Hitler during his trial . . . made it known that if he was not released forthwith [immediately], they would issue a public appeal that he be freed."[71] On December 20, 1924, Hitler was released. Photographer Heinrich Hoffmann had been invited by a Nazi publisher to drive to Landsberg to pick up Hitler, but prison officials forbade any

photography. Nevertheless, Hoffmann got his picture, according to Flood:

> With a terse greeting, [Hitler] stepped swiftly in to the car, and we drove off. . . . It seemed to me essential that a photograph to mark the occasion should be taken. . . . I suggested that we stop by the old city gates, where we would still retain something of the fortress atmosphere. To this Hitler agreed, and I took several pictures.

> We returned to the car, and I asked him what he intended to do next. "I shall start again from the beginning," he said decisively. "The first thing I want is office space. Do you know of anything in that line, Hoffmann?"[72]

As he had promised, Hitler immediately set out to rebuild the NSDAP. Far

Originally formed to serve as Hitler's personal security force, SS units evolved into the most feared branch of the Nazi organization.

from being discouraged by his arrest and imprisonment, he emerged with renewed energy and determination. Right away he arranged meetings with former party leaders and members. Within the year the first units of the SS—the Schutzstaffel—were formed. At first this group acted as Hitler's personal bodyguard, but over the years and under the leadership of Heinrich Himmler, a chicken farmer who had marched with Hitler in the Beer Hall Putsch, the SS "was transformed . . . into a state within a state, an army within an army."[73]

The Nazis Gain Power and Strength

The second volume of *Mein Kampf* was published in 1928, and by then the rebirth of the NSDAP was complete. In his conclusion to the book Hitler wrote:

> On November 9, 1923, the fourth year of its existence, the National Socialist German Workers' Party was dissolved and prohibited in the whole Reich territory. Today in November, 1926, it stands again free before us, stronger and inwardly firmer than ever before."[74]

Hitler was not exaggerating. The membership as well as the influence of the party was growing rapidly. German voters were electing more and more National Socialists to the Reichstag—the German legislature. Masses of German people supported the Nazis, but many of the country's respected citizens saw the NSDAP as a bunch of obnoxious, street-fighting roughnecks.

Their fears were justified; many party members were openly violent. Others had reputations of being womanizers and made no secret of their wild escapades with ladies. Ernst Röhm was openly homosexual, and there was talk that Rudolf Hess had similar leanings. But none of these reports seemed to concern Hitler for the moment. Author Langer reports that Louis Lochner, a journalist who interviewed Hitler, wrote that his "only criterion for membership in the Party was that the applicant be 'Unconditionally obedient and faithfully devoted to me.'" When Lochner asked about the shady reputations of some party members, Hitler is said to have answered, "Why should I concern myself with the private lives of my followers?. . . Apart from Röhm's achievements, I know that I can absolutely depend on him."[75] Hitler made it very clear that his associates' personal lives were of no interest to him.

His own private life also raised some eyebrows. There were those who claimed

---

Hitler's Passion for Geli Raubal

Robert Payne, in his book The Life and Death of Adolf Hitler, *explores Hitler's love for his niece:*

"Geli Raubal was the only woman [Hitler] had ever loved. . . . A blue-eyed brunette with alert, intelligent features and remarkable physical beauty, Geli appeared to have had nothing in common with her uncle. . . . She was [lively], frivolous, elegant, and aware of her beauty. When she entered a room, men turned their heads. She had no interest in politics whatsoever and wanted only to have a good time. . . . She had no talent at all for acting . . . and every passing thought or emotion could be clearly read in her features.

It was apparently this spontaneity that attracted Hitler to her, for it was a quality in which he was totally lacking. . . . He liked to have her at social functions and made no secret of his infatuation. [But] if anyone paid marked attention to her, he would fly into a rage and take her home.

Hitler was in love with Geli, but in his own peculiar way he was determined both to possess her and to keep her at arms' length. She was the ornament of his home and the delight of leisure hours, his companion and his prisoner. She had shown no desire to marry him, but he possessed an overmastering will. . . . So he kept her and held her at arms' length, afraid to advance and afraid to retreat."

that Hitler himself was homosexual, for he seemed to have little interest in women. The only one who did attract him was his niece, Geli Raubal, daughter of his half sister, Angela. After the death of Geli's father, Hitler made himself her guardian, and reserved for her the bedroom beside his own in the large Munich apartment in Prinzregentenplatz, where he moved in September 1929.

Despite Hitler's love for the girl, the two quarreled often, and some people said he harmed her physically. But the truth was never known, for on the morning of September 19, 1931, Geli was found shot to death at the Prinzregentenplatz apartment. There were rumors that Hitler had killed her himself in a fit of jealous rage. But more likely she committed suicide, frustrated by the demands that her overprotective uncle constantly put on her.

In the days after Geli's death, Hitler went into deep shock. Those close to him feared he might attempt suicide himself. It was then that his vegetarian eating habits began, for he could no longer bear the sight of meat. "It is like eating a corpse!"[76] he told associate Hermann Göring. For the rest of his life, Adolf mourned for his niece. He hung her photograph on his wall in Munich and later at his headquarters in Berlin, putting flowers beside it on her birth and death dates each year.

"Make That Man My Chancellor?"

Hitler recovered from the shock by throwing himself into his continuing quest for power. Not long after Geli's death he re-quested a meeting with German president Paul von Hindenburg. The elderly president's support was slipping nationwide as people's frustrations with the Weimar Republic increased. At the same time, the Nazis were fast becoming the largest political party in the Reichstag. Hitler was eager for Hindenburg to name him chancellor, a position as powerful as that of president in the German government, but Hindenburg refused. "Make that man my Chancellor?" he asked in disbelief when staff members raised the question. "I'll make him a postmaster, and he can lick stamps with my head on them!"[77]

Aging German president Paul von Hindenburg refused to grant Hitler's request to be appointed chancellor, a position equal in power to his own.

By 1932 Hitler was backed by the support of nearly fourteen million German voters and a private army of four hundred thousand.

While enraged by this rejection, Hitler also realized that, in the end, he was the one who held the key to power in Germany, for he had the support of the masses. With nearly fourteen million voters on his side, Adolf Hitler was the fastest rising political star in the German sky. Another key element to power was force, and again Hitler scored high: his private army of SA and SS now numbered four hundred thousand.

What he needed next was the support of key business leaders and people with money to put into his campaign. To gain this support, he began speaking to groups of businessmen, most of whom were worried by his socialist ideas. They had listened to earlier speeches where he talked about the good of the masses being more impor-

tant than the good of any one individual. Such ideas went against the businessmen's beliefs that private companies should be allowed to make money and show a profit.

Hitler was aware of their concerns. And so, with a different kind of charm than he used on the common people, he set out to win the approval of the businessmen. In January 1932, he traveled to Düsseldorf, the steel capital of Germany, to speak at a meeting of important industrial leaders. Looking like any other businessperson in the audience with his dark blue suit and black tie, Hitler spoke for nearly three hours, avoiding the loud, stormy phrases and gestures that he used in his speeches to the public. Another thing he avoided was any mention of Jews, for he knew that many successful businessmen were Jewish. As usual he told his listeners what they wanted to hear—that Germany could rebound from its depression to become the strongest nation on earth. But to succeed, he warned the business leaders, all Germans must work together toward one common goal:

> Today we stand at the turning-point of Germany's destiny. . . . Either we shall succeed in working out a common [political force] hard as iron from this [mixture] of parties, associations, unions . . . or else, lacking this [unity], . . . Germany will fall in final ruin. . . .

> If I speak to you today it is not to ask for your votes or to [ask] you on my account to do this or that for the Party. No, I am here to [tell you my] point of view, and I am convinced that the victory of [my plan] would mean the only possible starting-point for a German recovery.[78]

The businessmen were impressed. When the speech was over, the large crowd gave Hitler a huge ovation. He had convinced them that he was the one man who could lead Germany to world power, while at the same time protecting the interests of business. "As a result of the deep impression Hitler made on this occasion, the [businessmen] of the . . . region contributed heavily to [the] Nazi Party."[79]

One of the Most Popular Politicians in the Country

One troublesome technicality still blocked Hitler's path to becoming leader of Germany: He was not a German. Hastily the

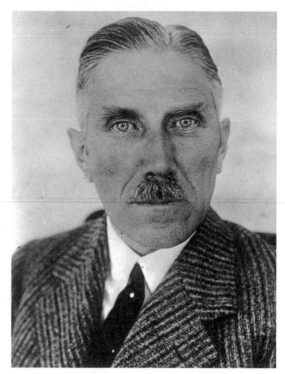

Despite enormous pressure to appoint Hitler to the post, Hindenburg chose Franz von Papen (pictured) to be chancellor.

Nazi Party machinery went into action to have him appointed councilor of the German state of Brunswick, or Braunschweig. It was a minor position and an unusual appointment, but it gave Hitler the appearance of a citizen. At the time no one questioned his status, for he was one of the most popular politicians in the country.

Despite Hitler's growing popularity, Hindenburg still refused to make him his chancellor. Instead he chose Franz von Papen, a man who had the support of politicians and government leaders. At a meeting in August 1932, Papen offered Hitler the position of vice chancellor and talked of ruling the country with a coalition government—one made up of leaders from each of the major political parties—but Hitler would hear of nothing less than full power for himself. Hindenburg remained firmly opposed; he considered the Nazis too wild and unruly to run a government. One of the president's advisers was at an August 1932 meeting that included Hindenburg and Hitler, and he wrote this report:

> Hindenburg, with a certain show of excitement, referred to several recent . . . clashes between the Nazis and the police, acts of violence committed by Hitler's followers against those of different opinions, [actions] against Jews and other illegal acts. All these incidents had strengthened [his belief] that there were numerous wild elements in the Party beyond [anyone's] control.[80]

Hitler left the meeting angry at Hindenburg's rejection of him; yet he was more determined than ever to have his way. Now the chaos churning within German politics began to come to his aid. The elderly president, although he clearly saw what kind of leader Hitler would make, could also see that his own grip on the country was slipping. His advisers, including his son Oskar, began hinting that he should get rid of Papen, for he was as weak and ineffective as the president himself. At the same time, Hindenburg was showered with letters—many of them from business leaders—urging him to make Adolf Hitler chancellor.

Late that November [1932], thirty-nine prominent businessmen . . . signed a letter [asking] Hindenburg to appoint Hitler Chancellor of Germany. These men were placing a bet on the NSDAP. They were confident Hitler's socialism [his belief that the good of

---

"I Will Tolerate No Opposition"

Newspaper editor Richard Breiting interviewed Hitler in 1931 and asked him, "Assuming you came to power, where would you find the brains to run the government . . . machine? The conversation is taken from Secret Conversations with Hitler.

"I am the master mind and my secret General Staff will produce the brains we need. . . . In the event of a successful revolution . . . do you believe that the German [middle class] . . . would refuse to follow us and place their brains at our disposal?

We give the orders; they do what they are told. Any resistance will be broken ruthlessly. I will tolerate no opposition. . . .

I have no wish to [kill] anybody. We need the [middle class's] brains to administer the new Reich. But we need only specialists, not intellectual [pretenders], and these specialists must obey orders blindly."

When Papen proved weak and ineffective, Hindenburg replaced him with General Kurt von Schleicher (pictured). This second rejection enraged Hitler and his supporters.

myself on the country; for this I am too proud."[82] He decided to meet his critics halfway and on December 2, 1932, replaced Papen as chancellor. In his place he appointed not Adolf Hitler, but Kurt von Schleicher, a general who had served under him in World War I.

Schleicher's appointment created chaos within the Nazi Party. Hitler suspected that one of his own men had betrayed him by helping to put Schleicher in power. Suspicion and mistrust clouded the NSDAP. Joseph Goebbels, Nazi minister of propaganda, saw a grim future for the party. In his diary he wrote:

> It is hard to hold the SA and the party officials to a clear course. . . . I sit here all alone and worry about many things. The past is difficult and the future is cloudy and dark. The terrible loneliness overwhelms me with hopelessness. All possibilities and hopes have disappeared.[83]

Even Hitler was discouraged and depressed as he often became during the holiday season. In a letter to a friend, thanking her for a Christmas present, he wrote, "Nothing will ever come of my dreams. . . . As soon as I am sure that everything is lost you know what I'll do. I was always determined to do it. I cannot accept defeat. I will stick to my word and end my life with a bullet."[84] But suicide was not necessary, for although he did not then know it, Adolf Hitler was soon to emerge from one of his darkest hours into a bright new dawn for National Socialism.

the masses was more important than the good of the individual] was a fraud and that, once in power, he would be the tool of [businessmen].[81]

Hindenburg was frustrated, discouraged, and too old to fight hard for what he knew was right. "I am ready to leave at any time," he told his associates. "If I don't have the confidence at home or abroad which I must have, I don't want to force

Chapter

6 "Forward with God!"

in John Toland,
Adolf Hitler

By New Year's Day of 1933, the German government was in chaos. The aging Hindenburg had lost control of the country, and Schleicher was proving to be a weak chancellor. In desperation some of the president's closest advisers—among them Papen—encouraged him to name Hitler chancellor. Although Hindenburg knew this would be a disastrous move, the old man was too tired to argue. "Is it my unpleasant duty then to appoint this fellow Hitler as Chancellor?"[85] he disgustedly asked those gathered in his office.

Hitler Becomes Chancellor

On Sunday, January 29, Hitler met with Papen and other Weimar government leaders to demand again that he be named chancellor. Otto Strasser, who with his brother Gregor had once been a strong Hitler supporter, reported on the meeting:

Hitler was exasperated. His voice was tremulous and his eyes watery. Nobody noticed that Herr von Papen had crept out of the room.

"I shan't allow myself to be pushed aside," Hitler shouted.

[Then] Von Papen came back, very calmly, and whispered something in [Hitler's] ear. . . . There was general panic. . . . Von Papen alone smiled secretly, while Hitler made a bold display of resolution. Was he not the strongest man in Germany?[86]

The "general panic" was caused by rumors that a military uprising was about to take place against Hindenburg, to keep him from naming Hitler chancellor. This was Hitler's signal to take action, and he declared defiantly that he would pit the SA against any military troops to bring the uprising under control. The panicked leaders, Hindenburg among them, saw no choice but to put Hitler in charge.

The uprising never happened, but the trick had worked. The next day, "as the clocks struck twelve," noted Strasser, "[Hitler] presented himself to Field Marshal von Hindenburg as Chancellor of the Reich. Adolf was in power. He had stopped at nothing to get it."[87] Hindenburg knew that his decision could mean doom for Germany, but he believed that Hitler was the only force that could stand up to the communists, who now posed a very real threat to the German government.

Many people besides Hindenburg also saw Hitler's appointment as a disaster.

After being sworn in as chancellor in 1933 (pictured), Hitler immediately set out to seize absolute power for himself and his party.

Erich Ludendorff, who was with the Nazis in the Beer Hall Putsch but had later become disgusted with Hitler, wrote a letter to Hindenburg on February 1, telling the president what he thought of his decision:

> By naming Hitler as *Reichschancellor*, you have delivered up our holy Fatherland to one of the greatest [rabble-rousers] of all time. I solemnly [predict] that this accursed man will plunge our Reich into the abyss and bring our nation into inconceivable misery. Because of what you have done, coming generations will curse you in your grave.[88]

It was a frightening prediction of truth. In Hitler's quest for power, "only one thing was still lacking," noted Otto Strasser, and that was "absolute authority."[89] It was not long in coming. Two of the conditions he demanded before being named chancellor were to be given much more power than any previous chancellor and to hold elections for a new government. As usual, Adolf Hitler got his way.

During the next month thirty-three new decrees, or rules, were issued that gave the Nazis supreme power. The legislature was dissolved. No political groups other than the NSDAP were allowed to hold meetings or to publish newspapers. Raids were conducted on the offices of Communist Party leaders, the Nazis' biggest political rivals.

The Nazis Storm to Power

On February 27 the Reichstag—the Berlin building that was home to the German legislature—burned to the ground. There were rumors that the communists had set the fire; others said Hitler was responsible. While the stories swirled, the Nazis used the fire to their advantage. The next day, under pressure from Hitler, President Hindenburg issued what were called Emergency Decrees for the Defense of Nation and State. These additional decrees made Hitler a dictator and gave his police the power to control the streets and public gathering places.

The elections Hitler demanded were held in March, and although nearly nine of every ten voters took part, the NSDAP received less than half the votes. Nevertheless, this slim plurality (more votes than any other party) was enough to keep the Nazis in power. Immediately Hitler made Joseph Goebbels his minister of propaganda and soon named Baldur von Schirach to lead the Hitlerjugend, the Hitler Youth.

That same month the Nazis opened the first of their many notorious concentration camps. Dachau—named for the Bavarian town near Munich where it was located—became one of the largest and most horrible of the camps. Habitual criminals, along with anyone who posed a threat to Hitler's goals or ideas—particularly his political enemies—could be sent here to do slave labor. Over the next twelve years, until it was liberated by American troops in 1945, thousands of people died under Dachau's brutal, inhumane conditions.

Only two months had passed since he became chancellor, but already Adolf Hitler held tremendous power. On April 1 he issued a boycott of all Jewish businesses, demanding that Germans not buy from shops owned or run by Jews. **Anyone Who Buys from Jews Is a Traitor!** read signs posted all around the Reich. **Buy**

The aftermath of the Reichstag fire. Hitler did nothing to dispel rumors that he was responsible for the fire.

Only at German Shops![90] The boycott lasted just one day, but it caught the attention of the world and struck fear in the hearts of Germany's Jews. The following month propaganda minister Joseph Goebbels urged students across the country to burn books that the government considered un-German. Naturally these included Jewish authors and others who disagreed with Nazi ideas. In Berlin on the night of May 11, musicians from SS and SA bands marched in a torchlight parade while twenty thousand books were burned at a huge bonfire in the center of the city.

Hitler's powerful propaganda machine was working its magic on the country. By the end of 1933 polls showed that 95 percent of the German people approved of Nazi policies. But unrest was brewing within the party. Hitler was upset

A storm trooper stands guard outside a Jewish business to enforce the 1933 boycott. The sign reads "Germans defend yourselves, do not buy from Jews."

"God Preserve Us"

Those who had been watching Adolf Hitler now saw their worst nightmare coming true. After a second interview with the Nazi chief, reporter Richard Breiting wrote his observations, which are quoted by editor Edouard Calic in Secret Conversations with Hitler.

"I am now convinced that, should he come to power, he will persecute the Jews. . . . He has no wish to hang them from the telegraph poles, as he said at the first meeting, but he will compel them to [leave]. . . .

I have the impression that he has no fear of the communists. . . . Undoubtedly he will have a showdown with communism. . . . He wants to submerge and crush everything like a tidal wave. And he wants to have done all this by his fifty-second birthday.

At our first meeting I was struck by his chin, which seemed to wish to crush everything. This time I observed his jackboots [military boots] which seemed to want to trample on everything. . . . God preserve us from this 'architect' and 'liberator.'"

The Night of the Long Knives was Hitler's attempt to get rid of anyone with power that he considered an enemy. Among those eliminated was the powerful leader of the SA, Ernst Röhm (pictured).

by the increasing size and demands of the SA, which threatened to become too powerful for him to control. Making clear the position he wanted the SA to hold, Hitler announced, "The *Reichswehr* [the German army] is the sole bearer of arms of the nation; the SA is responsible for the political education of the people."[91] This was not what SA leader Ernst Röhm wanted to hear. He thought his four million-member force should be the true army of Nazi Germany. Sensing Röhm's dissatisfaction, and recognizing the power he held, Hitler took steps to get rid of him, along with his followers. The Night of the Long Knives, which actually took place in broad daylight and was fought with guns, began on June 30, 1934. The order from Chancellor Adolf Hitler to the SS read: "Bring in Ernst Röhm, dead or alive."[92]

The Night of the Long Knives

When the Röhm Purge, as the bloody encounter was known, ended on July 2, Hitler reported that seventy-four people had been killed. In fact, many more than that probably died, many of them with no connection to the SA. The Night of the Long Knives (the Röhm Purge's popular name) was a "cleansing" of anyone whom Hitler considered an enemy of his plans, his policies, or his life. Among those killed were former chancellor Kurt von Schleicher and his wife. Ernst Röhm was arrested by Hitler himself and "allowed" to commit suicide in his jail cell; in fact, he was executed without trial by SS officers. Another victim was Gregor Strasser who, with his brother Otto, had earlier been a

A Brutal Dictatorship

American journalist William Shirer had a firsthand look at Hitler's rise to power while he was living in Germany from 1934 to 1940. He wrote his impressions of the rising star in his book The Rise and Fall of the Third Reich.

"There was much that impressed, puzzled and troubled [me] about the new Germany. The overwhelming majority of Germans did not seem to mind that their personal freedom had been taken away, that so much of their culture had been destroyed and replaced with a mindless [savageness]. . . .

The Blood Purge of June 30, 1934, was a warning of how ruthless the new leaders could be. Yet [I] . . . was somewhat surprised to see that the people of this country did not seem to feel that they were being cowed and held down by a [dishonest] and brutal dictatorship. On the contrary, they supported it with genuine enthusiasm.

The racial laws which excluded the Jews from the German community seemed to [me] to be a shocking throwback to primitive times, but since the Nazi racial theories [hailed] the Germans as the salt of the earth and the master race, they were far from being unpopular."

major force in the NSDAP. In recent years Gregor had disagreed with Hitler on important matters of policy, and leaders worried that he was trying to take over the party. Also killed in the Röhm Purge was Father Bernhard Stempfle, a Catholic priest who had helped to edit *Mein Kampf*. He knew much—perhaps too much, some said—about Hitler's personal life, and in particular the real facts behind Geli Raubal's supposed suicide.

To clear himself of blame in the Röhm Purge, Hitler issued a law on July 3, making all the killings legitimate. In speaking of "the tragic events of June 30, 1934," Otto Strasser wrote: "To keep himself in power Adolf Hitler used two instruments, propaganda and terrorism, the devastat-

ing effectiveness of which it would be idle [useless] to deny."[93]

Hitler Claims Total Power

Hitler's quest for total power took another giant step forward on the morning of August 2, when the aged president, Paul von Hindenburg, died. By noon, Hitler had announced a new law that he claimed had been approved by government leaders one day earlier. The law combined the offices of president and chancellor, which meant that Adolf Hitler was now the all-powerful, undisputed leader of Germany. Every member of the armed forces was required to pledge a new oath, not to support his country, but to support Hitler himself:

> I swear by God this sacred oath, that I will render unconditional obedience to Adolf Hitler, the *Führer* of the German Reich and people, Supreme Commander of the Armed Forces, and will be ready as a brave soldier to risk my life at any time for this oath.[94]

Now that he had the power he craved, Hitler began working to restore Germany's economy and find jobs for the millions of unemployed. One of his first steps was to expand the DAF (Deutsche Arbeiter Front, or German Labor Front), the government-run labor union that all German workers were required to join. Because the DAF was the only labor union allowed by the Nazis, it controlled the wages and working conditions for all German laborers. No longer could people go on strike or complain about hours, working conditions, or wages.

But most people were so glad to be earning a regular paycheck that few of them worried about the power held by the DAF. When Hitler became chancellor in 1933, six million people were out of work. Just three years later nearly everyone had jobs and a little money in their pockets. There was a sense of security and hope—a feeling the people had not known for many years. They called it "the German economic miracle." This miracle, said German journalist Sebastian Haffner, "was Hitler's most popular achievement":

> It is difficult to picture . . . the grateful amazement with which the Germans reacted to that miracle. . . . [It] dominated the mood of the German masses

during the 1936 to 1938 period and made anyone who still rejected Hitler seem like a [complaining] fault-finder. "The man may have his faults, but he has given us work and bread again" was the [common feeling] during those years.[95]

Along with work and bread, Hitler also made it possible for any German to own a car. At the 1934 Berlin Automobile Show, the führer unveiled plans for the new Volkswagen, the "people's car." Citizens could save for their cars by purchasing weekly government savings stamps at a very low price. At the end of four years they would have saved enough to buy one

Hitler (at back) developed a plan that made it possible for every German to own a Volkswagen, the automobile he dubbed the "people's car."

of the new little black cars. To handle the increase in traffic throughout the country, Hitler also introduced the autobahn, a system of four-lane roads that stretched across two thousand miles of German countryside. This novel idea in transportation became the model for today's high-speed interstate highways.

Next declaring that it was more important to feed the souls of men than their stomachs, the Nazis arranged a program of entertainment and vacations, to be paid for in part by the government. All German workers were required to help pay for this Strength Through Joy program by having money deducted from their paychecks. Hitler appointed labor leader Robert Ley to head the program, which offered adult education classes, music and theater productions, sports events, dances, cruises, trips to the mountains, and even vacations in other parts of Europe. At its peak, Strength Through Joy boasted twenty-five million members.

The Darker Side of Nazism

While their minds, souls, and stomachs were being well fed, the eyes of millions of Germans remained closed to the evil that was brewing in Hitler's cauldron. There were some who worried, however, and with good reason. Since 1933 Jews had not been allowed to hold public office, to teach, or to work in communications or farming. Within a few years, they were forbidden to run their own businesses or to become lawyers or doctors.

In September 1935, at the Nazi Party's annual Nuremberg Rally, the Nazis made public a new set of laws dealing with citi-

zenship and race. Under the Nuremberg Laws, Jews were no longer German citizens. Marriages between Jews and pure Aryan Germans were forbidden. Jews could not hire Aryan women younger than thirty-five to work in their homes. Increasingly the Jews found more and more services closed to them; even simple privileges like buying food were denied them in many towns. Across the *Reich*, or "nation," signs went up saying: **JEWS NOT ADMITTED, JEWS STRICTLY FORBIDDEN IN THIS TOWN,** or **JEWS ENTER THIS PLACE AT THEIR OWN RISK.**[96]

The Nuremberg Laws should not have surprised the world. Hitler had predicted

A sign forbids Jews entrance to the Palace Park. The anti-Semitic Nuremberg Laws stripped Jews of their citizenship and placed severe restrictions on their lives.

Racial Purity

In The War Against the Jews, *Lucy Dawidowicz quotes some of the "Ten Commandments of Lawful Self-Defense." She says this anti-Semitic propaganda influenced Hitler.*

"Thou shalt keep thy blood pure. Consider it a crime to soil the noble Aryan breed of thy people by mingling it with the Jewish breed. For thou must know that Jewish blood is everlasting, putting the Jewish stamp on body and soul unto the farthest generations.

Thou shalt have no social [interaction] with the Jew. Avoid all contact and community with the Jew and keep him away from thyself and thy family, especially thy daughters, lest they suffer injury of body and soul."

---

his actions many times in *Mein Kampf:* "The first task is not creation of a *völkisch* state . . . but above all elimination of the existing Jewish one." He also wrote of bringing to an end the power he believed Jews held over business and government:

> The end is not only the end of the freedom of the peoples oppressed by the Jew, but also the end of this para-site [all Jews] upon the nations. After the death of his victim [the common working person], the vampire [the Jew] sooner or later dies too.[97]

This was not the only warning Adolf Hitler gave the world. He also predicted in *Mein Kampf* a time when the German nation would need more living space:

National Socialists must . . . *secure for the German people the land and soil to which they are entitled on this earth. . . . State boundaries are made by man and changed by man. . . .* The soil on which some day German generations of peas-ants can [give birth to] powerful sons will [justify] the investment of the sons of today.[98]

Clearly, Hitler was saying that he in-tended to expand Germany's boundaries. The investment of which he spoke meant war and loss of life, but the German peo-ple failed to grasp his meaning. Adolf Hitler had foretold his plans; his blueprint was there for all to see. Unfortunately, few were looking.

7 Certain Signs of War

Berlin, March 7, 1936. From the diary of American journalist William Shirer:

> Hitler on this day has torn up the Locarno Treaty and sent in the *Reichswehr* [army] to occupy the . . . Rhineland! A few diplomats . . . think it means war. Most think he will get by with it. . . . Tonight for the first time since 1870 grey-clad German soldiers and blue-clad French troops face each other across the upper Rhine [River].[99]

The Locarno Pact was a peace agreement drawn up in 1925 among Germany, France, and Belgium. The pact said that a portion of the Rhineland—an area in southwestern Germany occupied by the French after World War I—was to be kept free from any military forces. Deliberately defying that agreement, as well as the Treaty of Versailles, Hitler ordered his troops to march into the Rhineland. Secretly he thought there was a good chance

In deliberate defiance of the Locarno Pact and the Treaty of Versailles, Nazi troops march into the Rhineland.

Residents salute German troops as they march through the Austrian town of Imst in 1938. Millions of Austrians supported the takeover.

the French might stop him, and he ordered his men to retreat at the first sign of resistance. But there was no resistance. Wrote Shirer the next day, "Hitler has got away with it! France is not marching. . . . Oh, the stupidity (or is it paralysis?) of the French!"[100]

The Need for *Lebensraum*

With bluff and bravado, Adolf Hitler reclaimed the Rhineland without firing a single shot. The French, who could have stopped him easily at that moment, instead sat idly by. Hastily Hitler assured the world that he had no more conquests in mind. In a speech to the Reichstag he said, "We have no territorial demands to make in Europe! Germany will never break the peace."[101]

This talk of peace was only another Hitler bluff. On November 5, 1937, he called a meeting of six of his top military advisers. For more than four hours they listened to him, "silent and uneasy."[102] Germany's biggest problem, declared Hitler, was *Lebensraum*, "living space." The country needed more living space, and he intended to find it somewhere in Europe. Army colonel Friedrich Hossbach took notes at the meeting. "There had never been [living] spaces without a master, and there were none today," Hitler informed the group; "the attacker always comes up against a possessor. The question for Germany ran: where could she achieve the greatest gain at the lowest cost."[103] Hitler made it clear that *Lebensraum* could be acquired only by force. But when? And where?

Those questions were answered just four months later when German troops marched into Hitler's homeland of Austria at dawn on March 12, 1938. It was the climax of the *Anschluss*, his long dreamed of "reunification of the Germanic peoples." For months he had been badgering, threatening, and intimidating Austrian chancellor Kurt von Schuschnigg to turn over his country to the Nazis. When

The retaking of the Rhineland came as a welcome surprise to Germany's lawmakers, says journalist William Shirer in his book Berlin Diary. *Hitler waited until troops were actually moving to tell the six hundred members of the Reichstag what he had done.*

"Now the six hundred deputies . . . little men with big bodies and bulging necks and cropped hair and pouched bellies and brown uniforms and heavy boots, little men of clay in [Hitler's] fine hands, leap to their feet like automatons, their right arms upstretched in the Nazi salute, and scream '*Heil*'s,' the first two or three wildly, the next twenty-five in unison. . . . Hitler now has them in his claws. . . .

Their hands are raised in [slavelike] salute, their faces now contorted with hysteria, their mouths wide open, shouting, shouting, their eyes, burning with fanaticism, glued on the new god, the Messiah. The Messiah plays his role superbly. His head lowered as if in all humbleness, he waits patiently for silence."

Schuschnigg refused, Hitler sent in troops to herd him and seventy-six thousand fellow Austrians to various concentration camps. Journalist William Shirer was in Vienna, the Austrian capital, and wrote this report at 4 A.M. on March 12:

> The worst has happened! Schuschnigg is out. The Nazis are in. The *Reichswehr* is invading Austria. Hitler has broken a dozen solemn promises, pledges, treaties. And Austria is finished. Beautiful, tragic, civilized Austria! Gone. Done to death.[104]

To complete his Austrian victory, Hitler called for an election to be held on April 10. The results, he claimed, showed that 99 percent of the people supported *Anschluss*, the NSDAP, and Adolf Hitler as their führer. While it was true that millions of Austrians did openly welcome the Nazis, there were many who saw the takeover as a disaster. Within months Austria had its own concentration camp at Mauthausen, located near Hitler's former home of Linz. Here, under a blanket of increasing terror, "the executions of at least 35,000 victims of the *Anschluss* took place."[105] This was the fate of the Austrians who had dared to oppose their new rulers.

Where Will the Führer Turn Next?

Jittery Europeans had serious reasons to fear the fiery little man with the Charlie Chaplin mustache. "There was no doubt where Hitler would turn next," wrote historian Alan Bullock. "He had hated the

Hitler receives an enthusiastic welcome from crowds after Germany's liberation of the Sudetenland from Czechoslovakian rule.

Czechs since his Vienna days, when they had appeared to him as . . . those Slav *Untermenschen*—'Subhumans'—who were challenging the supremacy of the Germans."[106] Czechoslovakian leaders listened with growing concern to Hitler's harangues against their government. He claimed the Czechs were mistreating Germanic people who lived in the Sudetenland, the part of Czechoslovakia that bordered southeastern Germany. Hitler encouraged the Sudeten Germans to break away from their country and threatened to attack if the Sudetenland were not set free.

Although Czech leaders were concerned, their fears were somewhat eased by an agreement they had with France and the Soviet Union. Surely, they thought, those countries would come to their aid if Nazi threats became real. But Adolf Hitler knew better than the Czech government what to expect from France and the Soviet Union, for he had amazing insight into

the minds and motives of his enemies. The French—as well as the British and Soviets—were, Hitler believed, too anxious to avoid war to step in and defend Czechoslovakia.

He was right. During the month of September 1938, British prime minister Neville Chamberlain and other Allied leaders met several times, hoping to work out a plan for the Sudetenland. By the end of the month an agreement seemed possible, but time was running out, and Hitler was not cooperating. "If these tortured creatures," he screamed, referring to the Sudeten Germans, "cannot obtain rights and assistance by themselves, they can obtain both from us."[107] He set October 1 as the deadline for Czechoslovakia to give up the Sudetenland or face attack, adding a warning that there would be no exceptions. In vain, Great Britain's frustrated prime minister begged for a little more time, telling Hitler, "I cannot believe that you will take responsibility of starting a world war which may end civilization for the sake of a few days' delay in settling this long-standing problem."[108]

Chamberlain should have believed it; England and France should have come to the aid of their Czech neighbors. On October 1, while the rest of Europe looked the other way, German troops marched into the Sudetenland, proudly proclaiming it free from Czechoslovakia and part of the German Reich.

The Horror of Kristallnacht

The Sudetenland was just another step. Hitler next turned his eyes toward Poland. In his never-ending search for *Lebensraum*, Germany's neighbor to the east was a prime target. Sensing what was to come, Poland enforced laws to restrict the entry of foreigners into the country. This move angered Hitler, and in revenge he ordered thousands of Polish Jews then living in Germany to be arrested and returned to Poland. But at the border Polish officials refused to accept the refugees, and they spent several miserable weeks living in a no-man's-land. Among the refugees who found themselves without a home was the father of Herschel Grynszpan, a seventeen-year-old student then living in Paris. Enraged by Hitler's order and his treatment of the Jews, Grynszpan walked into a government building in Paris, where he shot and killed a German official, Ernst vom Rath. Immediately the Nazis made Rath a martyr and a hero, and ordered *Aktionen*, "actions," to be taken against Jews all across Germany, with particular action to be directed at the synagogues.

The organizer of what became known as Kristallnacht, "Night of the Broken Glass," was Reinhard Heydrich, one of the most vile and fearsome Nazis, who had joined Hitler and the NSDAP in 1931. Among the orders Heydrich issued for the night of November 9 were:

> Business and private apartments of Jews may be destroyed but not looted. . . .
>
> The demonstrations which are going to take place should not be hindered by the police. . . .
>
> As many Jews, especially rich ones, are to be arrested as can be accommodated in the existing prisons. . . . Upon their arrest, the appropriate concentration camps should be contacted immediately, in order to confine them in these camps as soon as possible.[109]

As the organizer of Kristallnacht, Reinhard Heydrich ordered the destruction of Jewish homes, businesses, and synagogues, and the arrest of Jews for deportation to concentration camps.

"A Step That Sealed the Fate of His Country"

On the morning after Kristallnacht, Albert Speer, chief architect for the Third Reich, drove to his office through the debris-cluttered streets of Berlin. He describes the scene in his book Inside the Third Reich.

"Driving to the office, I passed by the still smoldering ruins of the Berlin synagogues. . . . What really disturbed me . . . was the aspect of disorder that I saw on [the street]: charred beams, collapsed [building fronts], burned-out walls—anticipations of a scene that [later] would dominate much of Europe. Most of all I was troubled by the political revival of the 'gutter.' The smashed panes of shop windows offended my sense of middle-class order.

I did not see that more was being smashed than glass, that on that night Hitler had crossed a [major barrier] for the fourth time in his life, had taken a step that [forever] sealed the fate of his country. Did I sense, at least for a moment, that something was beginning which would end with the [destruction] of one whole group of our nation? Did I sense that this outburst of hoodlumism was changing my moral [makeup]? I do not know."

A synagogue lies in ruins after being destroyed during Kristallnacht, or "Night of the Broken Glass."

When the destruction of Kristallnacht was over on November 10, Heydrich himself admitted that 7,500 shops had been looted, although the official figures reported only 815 shops, 171 houses, and about 200 synagogues damaged or completely destroyed. Officially thirty-six people were killed and another thirty-six injured, but in reality these figures were much higher. Some twenty thousand Jews were arrested and sent to concentration camps. It was one more major show of force by Adolf Hitler in what appeared to be his unstoppable rise to power.

In the aftermath of Kristallnacht, many Jews made plans to escape. Hitler's drive to make the country Judenfrei, "free of Jews," was working well. Of the five hundred thousand who had lived there when he came to power, more than three hundred thousand had left by 1939. But each year there were fewer places for them to flee to, for Hitler continued to grab more and more land in his expansion of the German Reich.

On March 15, 1939, German troops marched into Czechoslovakia to claim the remainder of the country. By doing so, Hitler was breaking his promise not to conquer any new territory, but the world was rapidly realizing that promises meant little to Adolf Hitler. Ranting and raving about the supposed crimes the Czechs had committed against Germany, Hitler demanded that President Emil Hácha order his troops to put up no resistance, or the beautiful capital of Prague would be destroyed. Upon hearing this news, Hácha fainted and had to be revived by Hitler's doctor.

German Patience Has Come to an End

On September 26, 1938, Hitler delivered a highly emotional speech, preparing people for the invasion of the Sudetenland. German patience over the Sudeten problem, said Hitler, had come to an end. Historian Robert Payne comments on that speech in his book The Life and Death of Adolf Hitler:

"The speech was notable for its high-pitched screaming tone, its deliberate falsifications of history, and its total [lack of mercy]. . . . It was in this speech that Hitler stated clearly, and with perfect dishonesty, that he had no more [land] claims to make in Europe once his claim to the Sudetenland was satisfied.

Hitler's maniacal rages were not pleasant to watch, and until this time few people had observed them. Sometimes high-placed Germans would whisper stories about Hitler hurling himself down on the floor in one of his rages, biting the carpet in his [fits] of anger and frustration. The *Teppischfresser,* or 'carpetchewer,' had entered mythology, but until September, 1938, few people seriously believed he was capable of such absurdities. During this speech it became plain that he was capable of anything."

German troops march into Czechoslovakia in 1939, breaking Hitler's promise not to conquer new territory. This defiant act demonstrated to the world that Hitler could not be trusted.

Immediately he called his generals and told them to comply with the Germans. Czechoslovakia was dead; Adolf Hitler had claimed another bloodless victory.

Hitler Turns the Spotlight on Poland

With all of Czechoslovakia now part of the German Reich, Hitler devoted his full attention to Poland. What he wanted was for the Polish government to turn over to him the city of Danzig, or Gdańsk, along with a strip of coastline known as the Polish Cor-

ridor, both of which had been part of the German empire before World War I. When Poland refused, Hitler exploded. Meeting with his military commanders on May 23, he informed them that Poland was to be destroyed and offered this rather empty reasoning: "For us, it is a matter of expanding our living space in the East and making food supplies secure."[110]

In August Hitler met with his top generals to explain how the invasion would proceed. He wanted to make it appear as if Polish soldiers had fired on Germans along the border and that the Germans had fired back in self-defense. "Whether the world believes it doesn't mean a damn

German minister of foreign affairs Joachim von Ribbentrop (right) meets with Soviet dictator Joseph Stalin. The two leaders signed a pact in which Germany agreed to divide Poland with the Soviets after Hitler invaded it.

to me," declared Hitler. "The world believes only in success." The führer then explained how his troops should behave, instructing his elite and fanatic SS Death's Head Units to "kill without pity or mercy . . . men, women and children of the Polish race and language."[111]

The destruction of Poland [is most important]. . . . The victor will not be asked afterward whether he told the truth or not. In starting and waging a war it is not right that matters, but victory.

Close your hearts to pity! Act brutally! Eighty million people [the Germans] must obtain what is their right. . . . The stronger man is right. . . . Be harsh and remorseless! Be steeled against all signs of compassion! . . . Whoever has pondered over this world order knows that its meaning lies in the success of the best by means of force.[112]

To ensure that his attack on Poland went smoothly, Hitler had to be certain that Russia would not interfere, so he sent his minister of foreign affairs, Joachim von Ribbentrop, to meet with Russian leaders. The pact that they signed confused and stunned world leaders. By its terms, each country promised not to attack the other. Neither the Soviet Union nor Germany would get involved in a conflict that the other might have with a third country. Nor would either become allied with countries that promised to threaten the other. To sweeten the deal for the Soviets, Hitler promised to divide Poland between them, along with the smaller, neighboring Baltic states that the Germans also planned to conquer.

Adolf Hitler now had what he wanted: a clear shot at Poland without any Soviet interference. The time was right; the stage was set; within a week, the world would be at war.

8 "Today Germany, Tomorrow the World"

in Alfons Heck,
A Child of Hitler

"The fault which destroyed Adolf Hitler . . . was his inability to stop," writes biographer Alan Bullock. Hitler had "everything to gain by waiting for a year or two before taking another step,"[113] says Bullock. But he did not stop. His successful takeover of Czechoslovakia in 1938 had filled him with pride and self-assurance and made him all the more eager to extend his military campaign.

"Hitler's War" Begins

World War II—what Bullock calls "Hitler's War"—began on September 1, 1939, at 4:45 in the morning. Near the town of Gleiwitz, or Gliwice, on the Polish border, German forces attacked a German radio station. But they made it seem like the attack had been made by Polish soldiers, even going so far as to dress German criminals in Polish uniforms, inject them with a poisonous chemical, and leave them dead on the ground to make it appear as if Polish soldiers had been killed when they attacked the radio station.

The man who arranged this great scam, SS leader Reinhard Heydrich, explained why it was necessary to concoct such a story. "Practical proof is needed," he said, "for these attacks on the Poles and for the foreign press as well as German propaganda."[114] The Nazis wanted the world to believe that Poland had started the fighting. Speaking at the Reichstag that day, Adolf Hitler expanded on the lie:

> Last night for the first time regular soldiers of the Polish Army fired shots on our territory. Since 5:45 a.m. we have been returning their fire! From now on, every bomb will be answered by another bomb. . . . Whoever disregards the rules of humane warfare can but expect us to do the same. . . . I will carry on this fight, no matter against whom, until such time as the safety of the Reich and its rights are secured![115]

Blitzkrieg the Germans called it—"lightning war," a massive surprise attack. With the speed of lightning, Hitler's forces overran Poland, pushing Great Britain and France to declare war on Germany. But their declarations did little to stop the Nazi wave; Hitler was determined to win another stunning victory. Believing that "front-line troops must be assured that their leader shares their privations [hardships]," the führer put on a uniform each day and went out to inspect his soldiers. "He rode in an open vehicle," wrote historian John Toland, "so the troops

(Left) Hitler declares war on Poland during a session of the Reichstag. (Below) German troops roll through war-torn Poland after their devastating blitzkrieg brought the country to its knees.

would recognize him, while his [assistants] tossed out packs of cigarettes."[116]

The technique apparently worked. By September 23 the German armies were tasting victory, and four days later Poland surrendered. Adolf Hitler now seemed unbeatable. Among the Nazis there was great rejoicing, but many of the German people did not share their führer's enthusiasm for war. In Berlin, reported William Shirer, the mood was grim:

> I was standing in the *Wilhelmplatz* about noon when the loud-speakers suddenly announced that England had declared herself at war with Germany. Some 250 people were standing there in the sun. They listened attentively to the announcement. When it was finished, there was not a murmur. They just stood there as they were before. Stunned. The people cannot realize yet that Hitler has led them into a world war.[117]

Resistance to the Führer's Decisions

The German people were not the only ones stunned by the prospect of another war. Some of Hitler's generals were also distressed by his moves. To make matters worse, hardly had Poland been conquered when the führer began talking of attacks on other European countries. This kind of thinking, the generals warned, was "both wrong and risky"; one called it "insanity." Instead of more aggression, they recommended "putting the war 'to sleep'"[118] by taking a defensive rather than an offensive stand. Germany did not have the necessary supply of raw materials or ammunition to carry on a long war, the generals predicted.

If the campaign should encounter bad winter weather, it would end in disaster.

General Alfred Jodl, chief of the Wehrmacht, German army operations, was worried by the military's resistance to Hitler's plan. To have the army at odds with its commander in chief was what he called "a crisis of the worst sort." He confided to General Franz Halder, who led the invasion of Poland and was scheduled to lead the new attack, that Hitler "was embittered that the soldiers are not following him."[119] This conflict with his generals was a problem that haunted Hitler throughout his days in power. Often they disagreed with him, and more than once they plotted against him. As a result, he became suspicious of them and often ignored their valuable military advice. Thus

Hitler, the Megalomaniac

Many people who have studied Adolf Hitler's personality say he was a megalomaniac: a person who suffers from delusions of greatness. In his book Hitler: A Study in Tyranny, *historian Alan Bullock says signs of megalomania showed clearly in a speech Hitler made to his top officers in November 1939.*

"I must in all modesty name my own person: irreplaceable. Neither a military nor a civil person could replace me. . . . I am convinced of my powers of intellect and decision. . . .

My decision is unchangeable. I shall attack France and England at the most favourable and quickest moment. [Violating] the neutrality of Belgium and Holland is meaningless. No one will question that when we have won. . . .

No one has ever achieved what I have achieved. . . . I have led the German people to a great height, even if the world does hate us now. . . . As long as I live I shall think only of the victory of my people. I shall shrink from nothing and shall destroy everyone who is opposed to me."

Hitler became a military dictator who often ran his war machine single-handedly.

And yet, even though they disagreed with him, many of the generals did admit that Hitler had an amazing understanding of military science. Said Field Marshal Wilhelm Keitel:

> He knew so much about the organization, arms, leadership and equipment of every army and navy on earth, that it was impossible to fault him. . . . Even when it came to simple everyday issues concerning the organization and equipment of the *Wehrmacht* and [related] matters, I was the pupil . . . not the teacher.[120]

And so, against the generals' advice, Hitler pushed forward to conquer Europe, targeting Norway and Denmark next. Following that he planned to attack France and the Low Countries of Belgium, the Netherlands, and Luxembourg. Not surprisingly these future plans also frustrated and distressed his officers. This was madness, they told him. But the more they balked, the more determined Hitler was to get started. At last, on April 9, 1940, German forces marched into Denmark and Norway. The smaller country surrendered after only four hours, but Norway held out for two weeks, doing considerable damage to the German navy in the meantime. Despite this damage, the invasion was a great psychological victory for Germany and it convinced Hitler, if not his generals, that he had been right and they had been wrong.

A Curious Mix of Moods

Spurred on by his success, the führer now turned his eyes west to the Low Countries. From his new command post called Felsennest, "Rocky Nest," near the Dutch-Belgian border, he readied himself and the twenty-five hundred planes of his Luftwaffe, the German air force. The attack on the Netherlands was another grand success for the Nazi war machine. In just four

A photo of a bombed-out Dutch city reveals the massive destruction the Netherlands suffered at the hands of the powerful German air force.

and a half days, the Dutch army dropped to its knees in surrender. But victory left the führer in a curious mix of moods, recalls historian Robert Payne:

> Hitler slept little during the first week of the invasion. By the end of the week his nervous condition surprised his staff, who found him simultaneously elated by victory and in a state of profound depression, screaming and abusing his generals, continually warning them of disasters ahead, afraid that victory might be snatched from his grasp at the last moment.[121]

Hitler's next goal was to capture the French capital of Paris, and he ordered his troops to press steadily southward. Again, many of his commanders disagreed. They encouraged the führer to keep troops in the north long enough to capture French and British soldiers who had been cut off by the German invasion, but Hitler refused. He was anxious to take Paris.

On June 14, 1940, he achieved his goal. It was a sweet day for the Germans, who had been so badly humiliated by the French at the end of World War I. In just one week the French surrendered, and by June 25 all fighting had ended. German propaganda minister Joseph Goebbels recorded in his diary the mood of that day, as well as his thoughts on what lay ahead:

> Call from the *Führer:* he is quite boisterously happy. Praises my propaganda work, which contributed much to the victory. Does not yet know for certain whether he will proceed against England. . . . But if England will have it no other way, then she must be beaten to her knees. . . . We must wait. We must carry on regardless. . . . England must

A Frenchman weeps as German troops march into Paris in June 1940. The surrender of France was a sweet victory for the Germans, but the tide of war would soon turn against them.

not be allowed to get off easily this time. . . .

> Now the guns fall silent throughout France. Gripped by the magnitude of the moment. A victory, such as we could not have imagined in our wildest dreams, is ours.

> Thanks to the *Führer!*[122]

Hitler's First Military Loss

Just as Goebbels wrote, an invasion of Great Britain was next on Hitler's mind. What he hoped was that Great Britain would surrender after seeing the speed with which German troops had overtaken France. In a speech meant for the newly installed British prime minister, Winston Churchill, Hitler warned:

German Advances, 1939–1940

SCALE OF MILES

0   100   200   300   400

NORTH SEA

NORWAY

SWEDEN

BALTIC SEA

ESTONIA

LATVIA

LITHUANIA

Northern Ireland

Germany invades Denmark and Norway April 1940

DENMARK

Danzig

IRELAND

Germany invades Low Countries May 1940

EAST PRUSSIA

GREAT BRITAIN

ATLANTIC OCEAN

London

NETHERLANDS

Berlin

Warsaw

POLAND

Battle of France May-June 1940

Dunkerque

BELGIUM

GERMANY

Paris

LUX.

WWII begins when Germany invades Poland September 1, 1939

SLOVAKIA

Germany and Slovakia

Allied Nations

Neutral Nations

German Occupation

Soviet Occupation

German Drives

Vichy

SWITZ.

AUSTRIA

HUNGARY

FRANCE

ITALY

RUMANIA

Danube R.

YUGOSLAVIA

Believe me when I predict a great empire will be destroyed, an empire that it was never my intention to destroy or even to harm. I do realize that this struggle, if it continues, can end only with the complete [destruction] of one or the other of the two [enemies]. Mr. Churchill may believe this will be Germany. I know that it will be Britain.[123]

The British people and their government stood strong, saying of Hitler, "His picture of Europe is one of Germany lording it over those peoples whom he has one by one deprived of freedom."[124] They made it clear that they did not intend to be lorded over by Adolf Hitler or the Germans.

Although he still hoped that the Britons would lay down their arms without a fight, Hitler began preparing his forces for Operation Sea Lion, the code name for the invasion of Great Britain. To Hermann Göring, chief of the Luftwaffe, he issued the order to wipe the RAF, the British Royal Air Force, from the skies. Crippling the RAF would clear the way for the German navy to invade Great Britain across the English Channel. Göring assured the führer that this would be no problem. To Admiral Erich Raeder, head of the German navy, Hitler gave the instruction to clear the channel of explosive British mines and replace them with German mines. There were also orders to cripple the British navy, but on this Raeder made no promises.

Nor should Göring have made them either. Beginning in July, and throughout the summer of 1940, fierce fighting raged in the skies over southern England. But the air battles did not go as Göring had predicted nor as Hitler had hoped. In each of the five phases of fighting, the Luftwaffe lost more planes than the RAF. The air war reached a climax on September 15, which Britons continue to celebrate as Battle of Britain Day, when the Luftwaffe suffered tremendous losses. Its efforts to clear the way for the naval invasion of Great Britain had failed. The disaster shook the confidence of the German people and the military and caused Hitler to change his plans for Operation Sea Lion.

On October 12 the führer issued this statement: "From now on until the spring, preparations for 'Sea Lion' shall be continued solely for the purpose of maintaining political and military pressure on England. Should the invasion be reconsidered in the spring or early summer of 1941, orders for a renewal of operation readiness will be issued later."[125] There was no "later." Operation Sea Lion had come to a disastrous end—Adolf Hitler's first major military loss. In analyzing his decisions years later, many historians agree that Hitler's failure to conquer England was the mistake that led eventually to his downfall.

"The Greatest Battle in the History of the World"

At the moment, however, the führer was busy with plans for a massive new campaign in the east. This was Operation Barbarossa, Germany's code name for the invasion of the Soviet Union. In December 1940 Hitler issued orders for a

The dome of St. Paul's Cathedral in London rises through the thick smoke left in the wake of the air battles over Great Britain, Hitler's first major military loss.

blitzkrieg attack on the very country with whom he had signed a nonaggression pact just one year earlier. Operation Barbarossa was to be completed by May 15, 1941. When it was over, Hitler predicted, the Soviet army would be destroyed. But, in fact, the invasion did not begin until June 22, a delay that brought disaster to the Wehrmacht.

In the beginning, Operation Barbarossa appeared to be a success, another of Hitler's incredible blitzkriegs. In the first days of fighting, the Luftwaffe destroyed nearly half the Soviet air force. Summer campaigns went well for the Germans, and much new territory was added to the *Reich*. During this time, Hitler remained publicly silent. At last, in October, he spoke to the German people from the Sportpalast, "Sports Palace," in Berlin, giving them a progress report as well as propaganda to build their enthusiasm for the fight ahead:

On the morning of June 22, the greatest battle in the history of the world began. Since then something like three and a half months have elapsed, and I can confirm one thing here today: Everything has gone according to plan. . . . Never during the entire period did we lose the [lead] for even one second.

We have not been mistaken about the smooth working of all the operations at the front. . . . We have, however, been mistaken about one thing. We had no idea how gigantic were this enemy's preparations against Germany and Europe, how . . . great was the danger, and how narrowly we have escaped the destruction not only of Germany but also of Europe.[126]

Hitler should have stopped there in his speech, for that much was basically true. What followed was not. "I can also

SS commander Heinrich Himmler inspects a POW camp in Russia during Operation Barbarossa. The operation called for the invasion of the Soviet Union, which violated the nonaggression pact signed by the two countries a year earlier.

say," he assured the crowd, "that this enemy is already beaten and will never rise again."[127] On this point, Adolf Hitler was dead wrong. Soviet troops had suffered tremendous casualties, and the Soviet military had lost enormous amounts of equipment and ammunition, but they were not yet beaten and they would rise again.

The German soldiers hung on through a long, bitterly cold winter. By spring Hitler had a new plan—one that his commanders opposed. Although the Wehrmacht was just twenty miles from the Soviet capital at Moscow, he wanted to divert some troops south to capture the city of Stalingrad. His generals protested that this plan would spread German forces too thin. When General Franz Halder tried to warn the führer about a possible Soviet counterattack Hitler fired him, and he soon found himself in the Dachau concentration camp.

General Franz Halder warned Hitler of the potential for disaster if the German army attempted to capture Stalingrad. His warning unheeded, Halder was fired and sent to the notorious Dachau concentration camp.

A Catastrophic Defeat

Hitler should have listened to Halder, but instead he held firm and ordered certain forces to head south. By November and December 1942, as Halder had predicted, the Soviets threatened to overcome the German Sixth Army. The outlook for German troops facing their second impossible Russian winter was bleak. Hitler, who was in Munich celebrating the nineteenth anniversary of the Beer Hall Putsch, failed to understand the seriousness of their situation. When he got the news that Field Marshal Friedrich Paulus's Sixth Army had been surrounded, the führer stood firm: There would be no retreat. He ordered Paulus to hold his ground. "Stalin-grad simply must be held. It must be; it is a key position."[128]

Just how Stalingrad was to be held, Hitler did not say. But Luftwaffe chief Hermann Göring assured him that the trapped German soldiers could be supplied by air. It was a promise Göring could not keep; the Luftwaffe failed in its mission. By February 1943, the Sixth Army could hold out no longer. At last, defying Hitler's order to stand firm, Paulus surrendered. The führer's insistence to fight to the last man had cost the German army several thousand additional lives.

The defeat was a catastrophe of the greatest dimension for Germany and a

Stress Begins to Take Its Toll

Russian soldiers defend a vital railway line against Nazi invaders. The Soviet campaign ended in bitter defeat for the Germans, and marked a turning point in the war.

turning point in the war. Hitler's reaction was rage: "Paulus did an about-face on the threshold of immortality,"[129] he fumed. "The man should have shot himself just as the old commanders threw themselves on their swords."[130] On February 3 Germany began a three-day period of national mourning for the soldiers sacrificed at Stalingrad. Businesses were ordered closed, and Chopin's "Funeral March" was played on national radio. The government issued an official statement saying that "the sacrifices of the Army, bulwark of a historical European mission, were not in vain."[131] Hitler's own reaction was silence, recalled Nazi architect Albert Speer. "In the future, [he] never said another word about the catastrophe for which he and Göring were alone responsible."[132]

The tremendous stress in Adolf Hitler's life was beginning to take a heavy toll on his health. During the Soviet campaign he had made his headquarters at Wolf's Lair, a cold, drab command post in East Prussia, just east of Gdańsk and the Polish Corridor. After the Sixth Army's horrid defeat, Hitler's doctor, Theodor Morell, recommended that he leave Wolf's Lair for a rest.

Morell suggested that the führer spend some time at the Berghof, his home on the Obersalzberg, a mountain in the Bavarian Alps near the German town of Berchtesgaden. Unlike the dark and dreary Wolf's Lair, the Berghof was a spectacular home, nestled in a beautiful mountain landscape. Hitler arrived there on March 24, 1943, and was seen by Morell immediately following a war conference. In his diary, the doctor wrote:

> I was called to the *Führer.* Complained of violent headache and a throbbing head. Temporal artery [on the side of the head] badly swollen. Looking generally tired and [weak]. . . . Took his blood pressure. It's 170–180 mm [high]! Gave him two intravenous shots . . . and two tablespoons of Brom-Nervacit and an Optalidon tablet.[133]

Hitler trusted Morell completely, but the balding, overweight doctor was not popular with the führer's staff nor among his fellow physicians. "He didn't eat," said one doctor of Morell; "he munched like a pig at a trough." When the same man commented on Morell's obnoxious body odor, Hitler snapped at

Hitler and Blondi

As the German military slipped deeper toward doom, Adolf Hitler spent more and more time alone. Nazi architect Albert Speer, in his book Inside the Third Reich, *recalls how the führer's depression drove him to the company of his dog Blondi.*

"From about the autumn of 1943 on, he used to [say] 'Speer, one of these days I'll have only two friends left, Fräulein Braun [his mistress] and my dog.'. . . That was the one and only prediction of Hitler's that proved to be absolutely right.

[During his] walks, Hitler's interest was usually focused not on his companions but on his Alsatian dog Blondi. . . . During conferences that often lasted for hours, or during meals, Hitler ordered his dog to lie down in a certain corner. There the animal settled with a protesting growl. If he felt that he was not being watched, he crawled closer to his master's seat and after elaborate maneuvers finally landed with his snout against Hitler's knee, whereupon a sharp command banished him to his corner again. I avoided, as did any [wise] visitor to Hitler, arousing any feelings of friendship in the dog.

[Blondi] probably occupied the most important role in Hitler's private life; he meant more to his master than the Führer's closest associates. . . . The dog remained the only living creature at headquarters who aroused any flicker of human feeling in Hitler."

Depressed over Germany's military losses, Hitler increasingly sought the quiet companionship of his dog.

The Nazi flag hangs over the Berghof, Hitler's spectacular retreat in the Bavarian Alps.

him, "I don't employ Morell for high fragrance but to look after my health."[134]

Morell got used to the constant criticism, much of which focused on the continual injections, tablets, and tablespoons of various medicines he prescribed for Hitler. To his critics Morell merely replied, "I give him what he needs." On the surface, the treatments appeared to be working, but Morell could see that there were deeper problems and he suspected Hitler's heart. Seeking another opinion, he wrote a letter to a heart specialist describing the condition of "a patient," whom he did not name. He described him as one "who is subjected to huge burdens and can hardly ever take a [rest]." Although the heart doctor must have suspected who the mystery patient was, he nevertheless wrote back, "I would urgently recommend three or four weeks' complete rest . . . and actual work must be cut

back to an absolute minimum."[135] It was advice that Morell knew his patient would never follow, so he continued to treat him with pills and injections.

Another condition that haunted Hitler through much of his life now added to his health problems. On May 30 Morell reported, "After eating a vegetable platter, constipation and colossal flatulence occurred on a scale I have seldom encountered before. These were followed by intestinal spasms." The severe gas attacks, which Hitler himself linked to times of "violent emotional upsets,"[136] caused him both embarrassment and pain.

Adolf Hitler's Final Solution

Military losses and emotional upsets took a terrible toll on Adolf Hitler's health, but at the same time they strengthened his resolve to win his other war—the war against the Jews. In *Mein Kampf* Hitler had blamed the Jews for the country's troubles and defeat in World War I: "If we pass all the causes of the German collapse in review, the ultimate and most decisive remains the failure to recognize the racial problem and especially the Jewish menace."[137] Now, twenty years later, his hatred burned even stronger. In a conversation with his private secretary, Martin Bormann, he made clear his plans for dealing with "the Jewish menace":

> On the eve of the war I gave [the Jews] one final warning. I told them that, if they [caused] another war, they would not be spared and that I would exterminate the vermin [Jews] throughout Europe, and this time once and for all. To this warning they retorted with a

declaration of war and affirmed that wherever in the world there was a Jew, there, too, was an . . . enemy of National Socialist Germany. Well, we have lanced the Jewish abscess; and the world of the future will be eternally grateful to us.[138]

Hitler's plan for lancing the "Jewish abscess" had first been unveiled on January 20, 1942, at a small meeting of top Nazis in the Berlin suburb of Wannsee. Although the words *mass murder* or *extermination* were never used at the Wannsee Conference, it was clear to those gathered what was meant by the term *Final Solution*. The plan called for genocide: the elimination of the entire Jewish population. Reinhard Heydrich, second in command of the SS under Heinrich Himmler, conducted the conference. During the meeting he used phrases like "resettlement of the Jews" and "deportation to the east" to discuss the program. Although Heydrich and Himmler were responsible for carrying it out, the plan was Hitler's alone.

How could one human being plan the elimination of millions of innocent people? Jewish historian Raul Hilberg says that Hitler convinced himself that the extermination of the Jews had long been meant to happen. "Once, at the dinner table, when [Hitler] thought about the destruction of the Jews," says Hilberg, "he remarked with stark simplicity: 'One must not have mercy with people who are determined by fate to perish.'"[139]

The Final Solution called for rounding up the remaining Jews in Europe and transporting them east on trains in cattle cars. They were shipped either to filthy, disease-ridden ghettos fenced in by wood, brick, or barbed wire, or to concentration camps where they were put to slave labor

Piles of clothing are a grisly reminder of the innocent victims who died at Dachau. Such concentration camps were used to carry out Hitler's Final Solution.

and starved. The darkest side of Hitler's plan took place at six specially built extermination camps—killing centers—located in Poland. Here, millions of Jews were put to death quickly and efficiently in chambers filled with a poisonous gas, their bodies burned in ovens.

As his defeats on the battlefield mounted, extermination of the Jews became an ever greater priority for Hitler. Often he diverted trains that were badly needed to transport troops and supplies to haul prisoners to the gas chambers instead. By mid-1943 thousands of victims a day were being resettled to death or concentration camps throughout the German Reich.

The blueprint for the Final Solution may have been Hitler's alone, but it could not have been carried out without the cooperation of high-ranking Nazis and thousands of SS guards who ran the camps. How could these men and women live with themselves while taking part in such horrendous evil? They eased their consciences by refusing to think of their victims as human beings. They shaved prisoners' heads and assigned them numbers in place of their names. Often the guards dealt with prisoners in groups or blocks, rather than individually.

Some handled the horror by going into denial; they refused to admit, even to themselves, what was taking place. Pur-

"I See No Other Solution but Extermination"

At lunch with Heinrich Himmler just three days after the Wannsee Conference, Hitler made his goal in the Final Solution quite clear. Their conversation is recorded in John Toland's biography, Adolf Hitler.

"One must act radically. When one pulls out a tooth, one does it with a single tug, and the pain quickly goes away. The Jew must clear out of Europe. It's the Jew who prevents everything. When I think about it, I realize that I'm extraordinarily humane. . . . I restrict myself to telling them they must go away. If they break their pipes [die] on the journey, I can't do anything about it. But if they refuse to go voluntarily I see no other solution but extermination."

A few days later, at a speech in Berlin's Sportpalast, he continued his attack:

"I do not even want to speak of the Jews. . . . They are simply our old enemies, their plans have suffered shipwreck through us, and they rightly hate us, just as we hate them. We realize that this war can only end either in the wiping out of the Germanic nations, or by the disappearance of Jewry from Europe."

Nazi guards shaved prisoners' heads, assigned them numbers in place of names, and dealt with them in groups rather than individually in an effort to dehumanize them.

posely they looked the other way. When confronted with reports of atrocities, they claimed no knowledge. This was ridiculous self-deception, Nazi leader Hans Frank said later at his trial, following the war:

> Don't let anyone tell you he had no idea. Everyone sensed that there was something horribly wrong with this system, even if we didn't know all the details. We didn't *want* to know! It was too comfortable to live on the system, to support our families in royal style, and to believe that it was all right.[140]

Just how many Nazi leaders knew about the Final Solution, and just how much they knew, remained in doubt long after the war. But, wrote British historian Alan Bullock:

> One man certainly knew. For one man [this] was the logical realization of views which he had held since his twenties. . . . That man was Adolf Hitler. . . .
>
> Himmler organized the extermination of the Jews, but the man in whose mind so grotesque a plan had been conceived was Hitler. Without Hitler's authority, Himmler . . . would never have dared to act on his own.[141]

9 The Invasion of Festung Europa

By mid-1943 it was clear that it would take a miracle for Germany to win the war. Adolf Hitler was one of the few people who still believed in that miracle. During a three-hour speech in July, says historian Alan Bullock, he displayed "a fanatical will to conquer." Germany must be victorious *now*, Hitler warned the world. "If anyone tells me that our tasks can be left to another generation, I reply that this is not the case. No one can say that the future generation will be a generation of giants. . . . This is the voice of History."[142] And so the weary soldiers, some of them just fifteen years old, fought on.

Despite Hitler's optimism, the spirits of the German people were sinking. They suffered a tremendous blow on July 24, when British RAF planes began bombing the city of Hamburg. In attacks that lasted ten days, more than forty thousand people were killed and nearly that number

Hamburg, Germany, after a bombing raid by the British air force devastated the city, killing more than forty thousand people.

wounded. Architect Albert Speer, now chief of weapons production for the *Reich*, described Nazi leaders' reactions to the bombings:

> The first heavy attack on Hamburg . . . made an extraordinary impression. We were of the opinion that [repeated] attacks upon another six German towns would inevitably cripple the will to sustain [weapons] manufacture and war production. It was I who first verbally reported to the *Führer* . . . that [more] of these attacks might bring about a rapid end to the war.[143]

This report was not what the führer wanted to hear. "Hitler was enraged" over the bombings, recalled historian John Toland. Believing, in his irrational mind, that all the world's evils were caused by Jews, Hitler now became convinced that the Hamburg terror raids "were a product of the Jews; he accused the leading British air commanders . . . of being Jews or part Jewish."[144]

Luftwaffe leader Hermann Göring saw the picture more accurately. It was time, he believed, for Germany to move away from an offensive strategy and become defensive instead. Göring predicted that a good defense would save German lives and property and give the Luftwaffe a chance to recover enough to launch a counterattack. Convinced that he was right, Göring went into the führer's headquarters to present his idea. When he came out, said one of the fighter pilots who stood waiting for him, "we were met with a shattering picture":

> Göring had completely broken down. With his head buried in his arms on the table, he moaned some indistin-

Luftwaffe leader Hermann Göring infuriated Hitler by suggesting that Germany change from an offensive to a defensive strategy, which he predicted could prevent Germany from losing the war.

guishable words. We stood there for some time in embarrassment until at last he pulled himself together and said we were witnessing his deepest moments of despair. The *Führer* had lost faith in him.[145]

Finally Göring composed himself, stood before his pilots, raised his shoulders, and spoke defiantly—far differently from his mood just moments earlier. The Luftwaffe had disappointed the führer too many times, Göring reported Hitler as saying. This new idea of a defensive strategy was totally unacceptable; instead he insisted that the Luftwaffe stage a counterattack. "The *Führer* has made me realize our mistake," said Göring with newfound confidence. "The *Führer* is always right."[146] But the pilots knew that Hitler was not right. They saw clearly that to counterattack could cost Germany the war.

Still at the height of their power, Hitler and Italian dictator Benito Mussolini are welcomed by Munich crowds in 1940. Three years later, Mussolini was overthrown by his own generals. This news devastated the German dictator.

Just a few days earlier Hitler had suffered another devastating blow when his partner in war, Italian dictator Benito Mussolini, was overthrown by his own generals. Mussolini had supported Hitler and National Socialism throughout World War II, and his overthrow came as a severe setback to the Third Reich.

With the ousting of Il Duce, as Mussolini was known, Hitler's morale at last began to show some signs of suffering. He still deluded himself that victory was possible, that the *Reich* would ultimately triumph. But by late 1943 it was evident, says historian Robert Payne, that the führer was beginning to have some doubts. "More and more during those icy winter days, while the snow fell on East Prussia, Hitler found himself pondering the day when the armadas of airplanes and ships would stream out of England." In a paper Hitler wrote on November 3, Payne detected "a shrill note of alarm and the sweat of fear":[147]

> The hard and costly struggle against [the Russians] during the last two and a half years . . . has demanded extreme exertions. . . . The danger in the East remains, but a greater danger now appears in the West: an [English] landing!
>
> . . . Should the enemy succeed in breaching our defenses on a wide front [in the West], the immediate consequence would be unpredictable. Everything indicates that the enemy will launch an offensive against the Western front of Europe, at the latest in the spring, perhaps even earlier.[148]

The D Day Invasion

Hitler knew what was coming; he just did not know where or when. On June 6, 1944, he got his answer. That day, along the northern coast of France, the greatest land and sea operation in military history unfolded. It was D day—the day the Allies finally penetrated Festung Europa, "Fortress Europe," so called by the Germans, who believed their hold on the continent to be invulnerable. Hitler was asleep at the Berghof when the attack began. General Erwin Rommel—the Desert Fox—who now commanded the coastal areas of

France, was also in Germany, celebrating his wife's birthday. The blood drained from his face when a morning phone call advised him of the landings. "I'll return [to France] at once!" he told the caller. In the chaos, the plan that Rommel had made for this day was never followed. He wanted German soldiers to counterattack right on the beaches as the Allies landed, in the hope of stopping or at least delaying the invasion. Later Rommel wrote to his wife, "If people had listened to me, we would have counterattacked . . . on the first evening and we would probably have defeated the attack.[149]

Albert Speer, chief of weapons production, arrived at the Berghof at 10:00 A.M. on D day, and spoke hurriedly to one of Hitler's aides:

"Has the *Führer* been awakened?" I asked.

He shook his head. "No, he receives the news after he has eaten breakfast."

This day so crucial for the course of the war had not . . . been at all a turbulent one. . . . In dramatic situations, Hitler tried to maintain his calm—and his staff imitated this self-control. It would have been [breaking the rule] to show nervousness or anxiety.

It was noon before the most urgent question of the day was decided: to throw [troops] in France against the Anglo-American bridgehead. For Hitler had the final say on the disposition of every division.[150]

History now hung on the führer's word, and at this very late and critical hour, Adolf Hitler made a disastrous decision. Believing that a second attack would soon happen at Pas de Calais, near the narrowest part of the English Channel, the führer refused to move troops from there to Normandy, where they were desperately needed. Despite his generals' pleas for

The Allies land on the coast of France under heavy Nazi machine-gun fire. The D day invasion has been called the greatest land and sea operation in military history.

The Hitler-Mussolini Alliance

The bond between Adolf Hitler and Benito Mussolini was strong long before World War II. In his book Hitler: A Study in Tyranny, *historian Alan Bullock tells how Mussolini's fall from power affected Hitler.*

"The news of Mussolini's fall, though it had long been foreseen by Hitler, came as a profound shock to the *Führer*'s Headquarters. Hitler never wavered in personal loyalty to Mussolini. In private he constantly referred to him as the one man to be trusted in Italy. . . . Now, at one blow, after more than twenty years in power, the Roman [Italian] Dictator had been deprived of office, unceremoniously bundled into an ambulance and driven off under arrest—without a shot being fired or a voice raised in protest.

The [meaning] was too obvious for even the least political of Germans to miss. The *Führer*'s own [reputation] was directly involved and the Nazis' embarrassment was shown by the silence of the German Press after the brief announcement that Mussolini had resigned on grounds of ill-health."

Hitler shared a strong bond with Mussolini, his friend and partner in war. The Italian dictator's fall from power caused Hitler to doubt the future of the Third Reich for the first time.

reinforcements to fight back the invaders on the Normandy beaches, Hitler refused, and the Allied invasion succeeded.

The defeat left Hitler "in a bitter mood,"[151] according to Bullock. He blamed his generals for failing to stop the invasion of Festung Europa. On June 17 he called a meeting in France with Rommel and other top commanders. In vain they tried to make the führer understand Germany's grim situation. Rommel even hinted that it might be time to end the war. But Hitler was blind and deaf to such suggestions. Turning on Rommel in anger he cried, "*Herr Feldmarschall*, it is not your privilege to worry about the future course of the war. It would be more appropriate if you occupied yourself with your own invasion front!"[152] It seemed to his generals that Hitler had become paranoid and mistrustful of them. Reported historian Robert Payne:

> For an hour during the afternoon all discussions were abandoned, while Hitler took a leisurely meal of rice and vegetables. Rommel observed that he did not eat until his food was tasted for him [in case anyone should be trying to poison him] and that two SS guards stood behind his chair. He was obviously in ill health and incapable of forming accurate judgments.[153]

An Assassination Plan Takes Shape

Believing that their leader had lost control of his senses, certain generals felt it was time to remove him from power. To accomplish this, they devised an assassina-

Erwin Rommel, Hitler's favorite general, assisted in a failed assassination attempt on the delusional dictator's life.

tion plan. This was not the first assassination attempt against Adolf Hitler. Well before the summer of 1944, several other plans had met with failure. Count Claus von Stauffenberg, a colonel who had been involved in some of those failed attempts, was now more determined than ever to overthrow Hitler and even referred to him as the "Master Vermin of the Third Reich."[154] Among those who promised to help Stauffenberg was Hitler's favorite general, Erwin Rommel. Rommel did not approve of killing Hitler, who he feared would look like a hero, but he did want to see him removed from office and put in prison. "I believe," he told the conspirators, "that it is my duty to come to the rescue of Germany."[155]

Hitler was living at Wolf's Lair in East Prussia, where a meeting with top leaders was scheduled for July 20. Stauffenberg's plan was to plant a bomb, concealed in his briefcase, in the meeting room. When he entered the room, he saw Hitler bent over a heavy oak table, studying maps. Setting his briefcase beside one of the huge table legs, he excused himself to make a phone call. When the bomb went off, exactly at 12:42 P.M., Stauffenberg was catching a plane to Berlin to begin the next phase of the assassination plan: the takeover of the German government while the Nazis were in chaos and without a leader.

But when he arrived in the capital city, Stauffenberg learned to his dismay that something had gone wrong. The plot against Hitler's life had failed again. The bomb had gone off, and four of the twenty-four people in the room were killed, but Hitler was not among them. Although Hitler was severely shaken by the blast, his right arm bruised and temporarily paralyzed and his hearing affected, he had no life-threatening injuries. Had the meeting taken place in the concrete bunker with its tight walls, where it was originally scheduled, Hitler and everyone else in the room surely would have died. But at the last minute it was changed to a flimsy wooden building that could not contain the blast.

Ruthless Nazi Revenge

Later that day Benito Mussolini arrived at Wolf's Lair for a scheduled meeting with Hitler. Fresh from the claws of death, Hitler told his Italian Axis partner that he was now "more convinced than ever that the great cause which I serve will be brought through its present perils and that everything can be brought to a good end." Mussolini, as usual, was swept up by Hitler's logic and manner of speaking. "After [this] miracle," he said, referring to the führer's having survived the bomb blast, "it is [unthinkable] that our cause should meet with misfortune."[156]

The two men were suffering from delusions of the highest degree. The great *Reich* that was supposed to have lasted a thousand years was in tatters. Military forces were in shambles. The German people, like many other Europeans, were suffering, starving, and desperate to bring the war to an end. But Adolf Hitler's megalomania had overcome him. He could not see that his dream was shattered, his power gone. Mustering his usual self-confidence, he went on national radio just twelve hours after the assassination attempt to reassure the German people that he was alive and well:

> If I speak to you today it is first in order that you should hear my voice and should know that I am unhurt and well, and secondly, that you should know of a crime unparalleled in German history.
>
> A very small clique [group] of ambitious, irresponsible, and, at the same time, senseless and stupid officers had concocted a plot to eliminate me and, with me, the staff of the High Command of the *Wehrmacht*. . . . This time we shall settle accounts with them in the manner to which we National Socialists are accustomed.[157]

That manner meant ruthless revenge. "There was a wild wave of arrests," reported journalist William Shirer, "followed by gruesome torture, [mock] trials, and death sentences carried out, in many cases, by slow strangling while the victims were suspended by piano wire from meathooks borrowed from butchershops and slaughterhouses."[158] Families and friends of the conspirators were sent away to concentration camps from which few returned. Field Marshal Rommel was—by Nazi standards—treated a little more humanely:

> On 14 October, two generals sent by Hitler arrived at [Rommel's] home. He was given a choice: stand trial and face charges of high treason, or commit suicide. If he chose the latter, no action would be taken against his wife and son. Rommel thereupon entered the car with the two generals [and] swallowed a poison capsule. . . . Those who saw his body noted the look of contempt on his face. Hitler had eliminated the single personality in Germany who enjoyed sufficient popular and military esteem to try to end the war.[159]

The Rapidly Aging Führer

In the weeks since the Normandy landings, the Allies had penetrated deeper and deeper into Festung Europa. On August

---

"I Am Grateful to Fate for Letting Me Live"

In an August 31, 1944, speech to his generals, Hitler maintained his insistence that Germany must fight to the bitter end. The humiliation of World War I, he insisted, must never be repeated. Parts of that speech are reprinted in Robert Payne's book The Life and Death of Adolf Hitler.

"I live only for one purpose, to lead this fight: for without an iron will, this struggle can never be won. . . . If necessary we shall fight on the Rhine [River]. Under all circumstances we shall continue to fight until . . . one of our damned enemies gets too tired to fight any more, and we'll go on fighting until we achieve a peace that will secure the life of the German nation for the next fifty or a hundred years, one that does not [destroy] our honor for the second time . . . as happened in 1918. This time I'm not going to keep my mouth shut. . . .

If my life had ended [in World War I], then I daresay that for me personally it would have been a release from worry, sleepless nights, and intense nervous suffering. A split second, and then one is free of it all, and there is rest and eternal peace. But I am grateful to fate for letting me live."

25 they reclaimed the French capital of Paris from the Nazis. The defeat dealt another blow to Hitler's shaky health. There was even some indication that he might consider suicide. "If these stomach spasms continue," he told his secretary, "my life will have no sense. In that case I will have no hesitation in putting an end to my life." And yet, he refused to consider bringing an end to the war. "Anyone who speaks to me of peace without victory," he screamed defiantly, "will lose his head, no matter who he is or what his position!"[160]

With the Allied clutches closing fast on the fatherland, Adolf Hitler returned to Germany from Wolf's Lair, on November 20, 1944. A short time later the rapidly aging führer addressed a small gathering of Hitler Youth leaders, among them sixteen-year-old Alfons Heck:

He spoke no longer than five minutes and what he said was meant for us, the Hitler Youth. We, after all, were his purest creation. . . . His voice, low and hoarse at the beginning, increased in volume when he mentioned the coming battles.

". . . We shall [destroy] this enemy . . . at the very gates to the Fatherland. This is where we are going to turn the tide and split the American-British alliance once and for all."

As we moved toward the door, Hitler held out his hand to each one. . . . [It] felt warm and sweaty, with little firmness. . . . I wiped [the tears from] my eyes when I walked down the steps. Nothing, I knew, would ever equal this day.[161]

Crowds of jubilant Parisians cheer American troops as they march in review after the Allies' liberation of France in 1944.

In a last attempt to save his crumbling empire, Hitler ordered a surprise German attack on Allied troops in the Ardennes Forest. The ensuing Battle of the Bulge (pictured) merely delayed the Allies from breaking through into Germany.

Hitler's generals now began preparing for their last major action of the war, a plan devised by the führer. On the orders that went out to each commander, Hitler added this note in his own handwriting: "NOT TO BE ALTERED."[162] So sure was he of the success of this plan that he told his arms expert, Albert Speer, "Everything else must be put aside for the sake of this. . . . If it does not succeed, I no longer see any possibility for ending the war well. . . . But we will come through . . . you'll see!"[163]

The Germans launched their surprise attack, known later as the Battle of the Bulge, on December 16 in the Ardennes Forest of Luxembourg. During the early days of the battle, Hitler's health was strong. Several entries in Dr. Morell's diary read, "No treatment!" or "*Führer* very well." But as losses mounted and the Wehrmacht began losing the ground it had gained, Hitler's health worsened. By Christmas Day gas attacks were giving him severe pain, and he had nervous spasms in his right hand.

Military losses were partly responsible for the decline in Hitler's health, but it was also clear that he had never fully recovered from the assassination attempt. According to Captain Heinz Assmann, who had a chance to observe the führer, "The rot had set in on the 20th of July and it was made only worse by . . . the questionable treatments and methods of Dr. Morell. . . . [To Hitler], who believed [fanatically] in his own mission and in Final Victory, the . . . realization of the [certain] defeat lying before us must have had a devastating effect."[164]

10 "The Chief Is Dead!"

Otto Günsche, in John Toland,
The Last 100 Days

Auschwitz, the Nazi hell on earth, was liberated by the Soviet army on January 27, 1945. When Soviet soldiers first entered the death camp, they could not believe the gruesome, grotesque scene that met their eyes. One of the SS guards, Pery Broad, had kept a diary at the camp, which he turned over to his captors at the end of the war. In it, he described those last days at Auschwitz:

> In the middle of January, 1945, Auschwitz was evacuated in wild panic. All prisoners who were able to walk were dragged off to concentration camps situated deep inside Germany.

. . . Those who were ill were left behind to their fate. . . . They would have been shot at the last moment, but all the SS leaders were scared and did not dare to give the order. In front of all the administration buildings . . . piles of personal documents were set on fire and those buildings, in which the greatest mass murders had been committed, the greatest in the history of mankind, were blown up.[165]

The guards' fears were justified; they knew that their Soviet captors would show them no mercy. Not only were the Nazis responsible, as Broad admitted, for some of "the

Auschwitz, one of the most notorious of the Nazi-run death camps, following its liberation by the Soviet army in 1945. The Soviet liberators were shocked by the gruesome sights inside the camp.

Curiously, those who bore the least feelings of vengeance against the Nazis were often the concentration camp survivors. Elie Wiesel was a teenager when American troops liberated Germany's Buchenwald camp on April 11, 1945. He describes the scene in Night.

"We were tormented with hunger. We had eaten nothing for six days, except a bit of grass or some potato peelings found near the kitchens. . . . At about six o'clock in the evening, the first American tank stood at the gates of Buchenwald.

Our first act as free men was to throw ourselves onto the provisions. We thought only of that. Not of revenge, not of our families. Nothing but bread.

And even when we were no longer hungry, there was still no one who thought of revenge. On the following day, some of the young men went to Weimar to get some potatoes and clothes—and to sleep with girls. But of revenge, not a sign."

greatest mass murders" in the history of man; the Soviets also blamed them for the deaths of millions of their countrymen and the destruction of their homeland during Operation Barbarossa.

Victory with a Vengeance

With a vengeance the Russian army moved swiftly west across Poland and East Prussia and in just two days had crossed the border into Germany. The enemy was now only ninety-five miles from Berlin, and Hitler hurriedly left Wolf's Lair to return to the capital city. From here he would witness and direct the last days of his Third Reich. The luxurious Reich chancellery, which housed the führer's headquarters, had been destroyed in recent bombing raids. To protect himself and his staff, Hitler moved into an underground, eighteen-room concrete bunker beneath the chancellery, which was small and uncomfortable compared to the lavish quarters he had occupied earlier. His aides and personal attendants, as well as the entire Goebbels family and staff, also occupied the bunker.

Speaking from there on January 30—exactly twelve years after he had come to power—Adolf Hitler gave his last radio address to the German people. It was peppered with ridiculous hopes for final victory: "However grave the crisis may be at the moment, it will, despite everything, finally be mastered by our unalterable will, by our readiness for sacrifice and by our abilities." Later that day he spoke to his officers, reminding them that Germany had surrendered too soon in World War I and that he would not allow the same thing to happen again. This time, he warned, "We must not surrender five minutes before midnight!"[166]

But Hitler's words went unheeded. There was no longer anything the führer or anyone else could do to save Germany. From February 4 through 9, Allied leaders met at Yalta, a city on the Black Sea in the Soviet Union, to plan their final moves of World War II in Europe. The leaders—who included British prime minister Winston Churchill, American president Franklin D. Roosevelt, and Soviet dictator Joseph Stalin—predicted that Germany would collapse about July 1. They were wrong; the end came sooner.

The Rhine—Germany's river of fate, where Hitler had sworn his troops would turn back the enemy—was crossed by the Allies on March 7. When he heard that American soldiers had set foot on sacred German soil, Hitler was enraged. He demanded that his troops fight back at all costs: "Anyone captured without being wounded or without having fought to the limit of his powers has forfeited his honor," he warned his men. "He is expelled from the fellowship of decent and brave soldiers. His dependents [family] will be held responsible."[167]

Still Hitler's hopeless optimism hung on. Shortly after the Rhine River crossing, SS general Ernst Kaltenbrunner entered the führer's office and found him standing over a large scale model of Linz, Austria. The town where Hitler had once strolled the streets with his friend Kubizek, making architectural sketches, had been severely damaged during the war. The model was of a new Linz, Hitler explained, the one he planned to rebuild. "Believe me," he told Kaltenbrunner, "if I were not convinced that I'll build up Linz again with your help, as you see it in this model here, I would blow my brains out this very day. *You must have faith.* I still have ways and means of bringing the war to a victorious conclusion." These were the words of a man who had lost his grip on reality but who still

Winston Churchill, Franklin Roosevelt, and Joseph Stalin (left to right) meet at Yalta to plot a strategy to end the war and clinch the Allied victory.

held an amazing grip on the people of Germany. Wrote historian John Toland, "Like so many others, Kaltenbrunner walked out of the *Führer's* office with new hope. In five minutes Hitler had convinced him that victory was still possible."[168]

The Twilight of the Third Reich

But it was not possible. Götterdämmerung, "twilight of the gods"—the violent collapse of a regime—had arrived. Allied forces from the west and Russian troops from the east were squeezing the last life out of Adolf Hitler's Reich. Beginning March 18 the Allies launched massive bombing raids against the German cities of Frankfurt and Berlin. Angry and deranged, Hitler now ordered his leaders to carry out a scorched earth policy. This order called for destroying German factories, communications centers, transportation facilities—anything that might help the Allies as they moved in on the fatherland. In Hitler's words:

> Every opportunity . . . to inflict the most lasting possible damage on the enemy's striking power must be used to the utmost. It is a mistake to believe that when we win back the lost territories . . . we will be able to retrieve and use these transportation, communications, production and supply facilities that have not been destroyed . . . ; when the enemy withdraws he will leave us only scorched earth and will show no consideration for the welfare of the population.[169]

Massive Allied bombing raids inflicted a heavy toll on Germany, as evidenced by this 1945 photo of the once glorious city of Nuremberg, site of the spectacular Nazi rallies.

The last ray of hope for the Nazis occurred on April 12, 1945, when American president Franklin D. Roosevelt died. Although polio had crippled him from the waist down at age thirty-nine, Roosevelt had gone on to lead the United States in its fight against Hitler's evil empire. His

Hitler spent his final days in the company of his longtime mistress, Eva Braun.

death from a brain hemorrhage brought shock and sadness to people around the world. But not to the Nazis. Berlin was burning when the news reached propaganda minister Joseph Goebbels. "Bring out our best champagne!" he shouted. "And get me the Führer on the telephone."[170]

On the line he congratulated Hitler, saying, "It is written in the stars that the second half of April will be the turning point for us." Reporter William Shirer described the scene in Hitler's underground bunker as having the "atmosphere of a lunatic asylum, with cabinet ministers . . . grasping at the readings of the stars and rejoicing amidst the flames of the burning capital in the death of the American President as a sure sign that the Almighty would now rescue the Third Reich."[171]

The Führer's Last Birthday

It was not the Almighty, but Hitler's longtime mistress who tried, in those final hopeless days, to come to his rescue. Eva Braun did not propose to save the Third Reich, but she did intend to die with the man whose company she had kept faithfully since 1932. Publicly Hitler had made few references to his relationship with Eva, but privately "she brought to him her youth, her freshness, and a natural elegance. . . . She was the one woman he constantly returned to, and she remained his mistress for the rest of his life."[172] Now, as Hitler's empire collapsed all around him, Eva arrived in Berlin to be with him. "[He] pretended to be angry at her sudden appearance and made a show of

The Woman in Hitler's Life

In his last, desperate hours, Hitler made his longtime mistress, Eva Braun, his wife. Hitler had spent little time or affection on her. Eva released her frustrations in her diary. This excerpt is from the entries of May 10 and 28, 1935, which are recorded in Robert Payne's book The Life and Death of Hitler.

"The weather is so wonderful, and I the mistress of the greatest man in Germany and in the world, am sitting here gazing at the sun through a window. How can he have so little understanding as to let me remain here, bowing to strangers. . . .

I have just sent him the crucial letter. . . . If I don't get an answer before this evening, I'll take 25 pills and gently fall asleep into another world. He has so often told me he is madly in love with me, but what does that mean when I haven't had a good word from him in three months?

God, I am afraid he won't give me his answer today. If only somebody would help—it is all so terribly depressing. Perhaps my letter reached him at an inopportune moment. Perhaps I should not have written. Anyway, the uncertainty is more terrible than a sudden ending of it all. I have made up my mind to take 35 pills this time, and it will be 'dead certain.'"

Despite her frustration over Hitler's lack of time and affection for her, Eva Braun remained devoted to the man that she described as "the greatest man in Germany and in the world."

scolding her," recalled Traudl Junge, one of Hitler's secretaries, "but all that first evening he repeated how proud he was of *Fräulein* Braun's devotion."[173]

On April 20, Hitler's fifty-sixth birthday, a strange mix of visitors came and went from the bunker to wish him well. On this, the last day of the führer's public appearances, he received a group of Hitler Youth, the organization of which he was so proud. He thanked them for their service to the Reich, encouraged them to keep fighting, and decorated them for their bravery. Although most of them knew that the end was very near, they listened while Hitler talked optimistically of destroying the Russians at the very gates of the capital.

In truth, Berlin was all that remained of the Third Reich. As bombs rained around the bunker, Hitler's faithful comrades urged him to flee the capital, but he refused. He had one final plan in mind. The next day he ordered the last all-out attack by German troops in Berlin. "Any commanding officer who keeps men back," he ordered, "will forfeit his life within five hours." Turning to one of his commanders, he threatened, "You will guarantee with your head that absolutely every man is employed."[174]

Despite the führer's threats, the attack never took place. Hitler simply did not realize how desperate the situation was outside the bunker. The only people left to defend the Reich were wounded and exhausted soldiers, old men, and young boys. When he learned the next day that his orders had not been carried out, Hitler was furious. Historian Hugh Trevor-Roper interviewed several people who were with Hitler in the bunker that day. They described a bizarre scene:

[Hitler] shrieked that he had been deserted; he railed at the Army; he denounced all traitors; he spoke of universal treason, failure, corruption, and lies; and then, exhausted, he declared that the end had come. At last, and for the first time, he despaired of his mission. All was over; the Third Reich was a failure, and its author had nothing left to do but to die. . . . He would stay in Berlin and there meet the end when it came.[175]

The Last Defense of the German Reich

The end was not long in coming. Defense of the Third Reich now lay in the hands of a thousand teenage Hitler Youth members, most of whom would perish for and with their führer. In the bunker Albert Speer reported that a strange, cold calm settled over Hitler. After a long day of meetings and talks with his advisers, he had gone to bed, but by 3 A.M. he was awake, and Speer sent word that he would like to say goodbye to his führer—for the last time.

I was afraid that I would not be able to control myself at our parting. Trembling, the prematurely aged man stood before me for the last time; the man to whom I had dedicated my life twelve years before. I was both moved and confused. For his part, he showed no emotion when we confronted one another. His words were as cold as his hand: "So, you're leaving? Good. *Auf Wiedersehen*." No regards to my family, no wishes, no thanks, no farewell. For

Condemning the Jews to the End

In Hitler's "Political Testament," written shortly before his death, he still blamed the Jews for all that had happened in Europe. George Stein reprinted parts of the testament in his book Hitler: Great Lives Observed.

"It is not true that I or anybody else in Germany, wanted war in 1939. It was wanted . . . by those . . . who either were of Jewish origin or worked for Jewish interests. . . . Centuries will pass, but from the ruins of our towns and monuments hatred of those . . . responsible will always grow anew, those whom we have to thank for all this: International Jewry and its helpers! . . .

I . . . left no doubt that if the peoples of Europe were once more to be treated as mere shares to be bought and sold by the . . . financial [plotters], then the responsibility would be shared by . . . the real guilty party in this murderous struggle: Jewry! . . .

Above all, I [ask] the leaders of the nation and those under them to uphold the racial laws to their full extent and to oppose [without mercy] the universal poisoner of all peoples, International Jewry."

a moment I lost my composure, said something about coming back. But he could easily see that it was a white lie, and turned his attention to something else. I was dismissed. . . .

Such was my last visit to the Chancellery. Years ago I had built it—full of plans, prospects, and dreams for the future. Now I was leaving the ruins of my building, and of the most significant years of my life.[176]

Speer's goodbye may have been cold, but it was not as shocking to him as was Hermann Göring's parting from Hitler. Göring had left Berlin for the Obersalzberg, along with many other top Nazis who had decided to abandon the capital. There Göring got word that Hitler had de-

cided to remain in the Berlin bunker. He also heard rumors that the führer had lost his senses and might even be dead. Hurriedly the Luftwaffe chief composed a telegram, reminding Hitler of a decree he had made four years earlier. The decree said that if the time ever came when Hitler could no longer rule effectively, the leadership of the Reich would pass to Göring, as second in command. In Göring's mind, the time had come. He advised the führer that if he did not receive a response by ten o'clock that evening, he would take over power and "act for the best interests of our country and our people. You know," Göring concluded, "what I feel for you in this gravest hour of my life. Words fail me to express myself. May God protect you, and speed you quickly here [to the

Bombers of the mighty German Luftwaffe fly in formation over Nuremberg in 1936. Hitler blamed Hermann Göring for the ultimate failure of the air force.

Berghof] in spite of all. Your loyal, *Hermann Göring.*"[177]

The telegram caused a new rage of fury in the bunker. Hitler accused Göring of committing high treason. He ordered him arrested, along with all other top staff then staying at the Berghof, and gave him the choice of resigning or being put to death. Göring chose the first. But the real reason behind Hitler's rage, says historian Trevor-Roper, was that he blamed Göring for "the ruin of the *Luftwaffe.*"[178] It was true; many Luftwaffe officers did agree that Göring was personally responsible for the failure of the air force. Hitler now ac-

cused him of failing to coordinate proper air defense of the Reich in its hour of greatest need.

By April 25, with Berlin completely surrounded and the Berghof being bombarded, Hitler sent a final message to his friend, Benito Mussolini. "The struggle for our survival is at its height," he said, and he blamed "the armies of Jewry" for creating "chaos in our continent."[179] The next day Mussolini was dead, shot and killed along with his mistress by Italian rebels as the two tried to flee the country. Their bodies were hung upside down in Milan's public square for all to view.

A Short-Lived Marriage

Hitler, sensing that his own end was near, named navy admiral Karl Dönitz as his successor to lead the Reich. He then retreated to his office to prepare his "Private Will" and "Political Testament." In his will, he wrote of his relationship with Eva Braun:

> Since I did not feel that I could accept the responsibility of marriage during the years of struggle, I have decided now, before the end of my earthly career, to take as my wife the girl who, after many years of loyal friendship, came of her own free will to this city . . . in order to share my fate with me. At her own request she goes to her death with me as my wife. Death will compensate us for what we were both deprived of by my labors in the service of my people.[180]

Just before dictating the will to his secretary, Adolf had married Eva. Despite heavy shelling outside the bunker, the couple exchanged vows and received the congratulations of those still present. Following the ceremony they retired to their rooms for a champagne wedding breakfast.

The next morning, April 30, having put in order his final business affairs, Hitler gave instructions for his faithful dog, Blondi, to be poisoned. By noon military reports from his generals were very grim, but "Hitler received these reports without emotion."[181] After eating lunch with his secretaries and cook and giving a final handshake to Joseph Goebbels and his remaining staff, Hitler went with Eva to their rooms.

Those present in the bunker reported hearing a single shot fired at approximately 3:30 P.M. A few moments later SS leader Otto Günsche entered Hitler's suite and found his body on the sofa, soaked in blood, a bullet through his head. Beside him lay Eva's body; she had swallowed a capsule of poison. Running from the room, Günsche stammered, "The Chief is dead!"[182] Then, with the help of others in the bunker, he carried the bodies up four flights of stairs to the chancellery garden, following the instructions in Hitler's will:

> My wife and I choose to die in order to escape the shame of deposition [being removed from office] or capitulation [surrender]. It is our wish that our

Hitler named navy admiral Karl Donitz as his successor shortly before taking his own life.

An American soldier surveys the wreckage of the room in which Hitler and Eva Braun committed suicide in order to escape the shame of deposition or surrender.

bodies be burned immediately, here where I have performed the greater part of my daily work during the twelve years I served my people.[183]

SS officers carried the bodies into the garden, laid them side by side, and doused them with gasoline. "They were at once enveloped in flame," witnesses reported. "The mourners stood to attention, gave the Hitler salute, and withdrew again into the Bunker, where they [disappeared]." In the confusion that followed, it was not known exactly what became of the bones. "It is sad," remarked one of the guards, "that none of the officers seems to worry about the *Führer's* body. I am proud that I alone know where he is."[184] But with Russian shells falling all around, the guard was soon forced to take cover, and as a result, no one ever knew what happened to Hitler's and Eva Braun's remains. Historians have said that the available gasoline would not have been enough to destroy the bones, but the bones were never found. On May 7, 1945, just one week after the führer's death, Germany surrendered to the Allies. World War II in Europe was over. Adolf Hitler, along with his Thousand-Year Reich, had disappeared into the ashes.

Chapter

11 The World Looks Back on Adolf Hitler

The remains of Adolf Hitler's body were never found. But the legacy of hatred and violence that he spread will never be forgotten. Today when anti-Semitism erupts, when racist attacks occur, when corrupt governments victimize innocent people, the world remembers Adolf Hitler and the Nazis. His name is synonomous with evil.

More than half a century after his death, people still ponder why and how Hitler and the Nazis were able to gain such tremendous control over the world. "No one, I think," wrote historian Hugh Trevor-Roper, "can have read this account of life in a monkey-house without asking at least two questions . . . : how did such monkeys succeed in seizing and retaining power . . . and how did they so nearly win the war?"[185] To the first question he answers:

> The Germans accepted [Hitler] as the Messiah for whom they were waiting, and in the hours of his apparent success they sacrificed their political institutions to him; for they believed not in them, but in the man.[186]

On the strength of his personality, Hitler created a colossal empire that totally consumed one continent and severely threatened two others. But it was a weakness in his character that ultimately destroyed that empire and caused him to lose the war, Trevor-Roper believes:

> The answer to the [second] question . . . is then, that they did not win the war, or nearly. What nearly won

Hitler took the stage in the right place at the right time, and on the strength of his personality created one of history's most evil empires.

the war was German industry and the German army. . . . What lost it was the unchecked development of dictatorship, [to] which the German people [gave in], even to the end, through a fatal political tradition.[187]

Germany: The Perfect Breeding Ground for Nazism

That "fatal political tradition" was a trait the German people had shown before. Their attraction for charismatic and often violent leaders had led them down paths of evil at other times in their history. One of the first was Attila the Hun, the barbaric leader of a warlike tribe that roamed central Europe in the fifth century. This fascination with warmongers and power-hungry leaders continued off and on over

several centuries. By the late 1800s, when Hitler was born, Otto von Bismarck, the Iron Chancellor, ruled Germany. Bismarck had united the German states into one empire—the second Reich—by using aggression and force, and by treating the people who worked for him like slaves. In a speech to the German people he proclaimed, "The great issues of the day will not be settled by [rules] and votes . . . but by blood and iron."[188] It was a prophecy that Adolf Hitler would also make come true.

How could a country that produced such superb writers, musicians, and scientists as Goethe, Bach, and Einstein allow itself to be taken over by such barbarians? Historian Alan Bullock says that Germany was a perfect breeding ground for Nazism. He agrees that in their "fatal political tradition" the German people valued power, glory, strength, and national pride, and were willing to follow—without question—

Adolf Hitler: The Great?

In his book Adolf Hitler: A Short Biography, *writer Helmut Heiber raises the interesting question, "What if Adolf Hitler had died on, say, October 8, 1938?" Heiber is quoted in George Stein's book,* Hitler: Great Lives Observed.

"Who would then have died: the liberator from the horrors of unemployment . . . , the destroyer of the chains of [the Treaty of] Versailles, the architect of Greater Germany—in short, Adolf Hitler the Great, one of the outstanding figures in German history!

And whatever the policy of his successors, they would either . . . have followed the path which he had traced for them or . . . squandered the inheritance of [Hitler] the Genius. But Hitler did not die in 1938. . . . [Instead his *Reich*] cost Europe 36 million dead and it cost German history a hero who might otherwise possibly have been [called] its greatest statesman."

Germany's intense patriotism, its love of order and strong government, and its need for a scapegoat at a time of national suffering all combined to make it an ideal breeding ground for Nazism.

those leaders who promised to deliver. Says Bullock:

> Nazism was not some terrible accident which fell upon the German people out of a blue sky. It was rooted in their history. . . . Hitler's career may be described as [the highest level of] . . . national [pride], militarism, [respect for authority], the worship of success and force, the [praise] of the State.[189]

The German people's love of order, organization, and strong government may help to explain why they followed a leader like Hitler. But what about the Nazis' darker side? How could a nation of civilized people ignore their government's evil treatment of Jews, Gypsies, Jehovah's Witnesses, and other non-Aryans? Jewish Holocaust survivor Primo Levi tries to answer this question at the end of his book *Survival in Auschwitz*. He points out that anti-Semitism had been around for centuries, but that it "was heightened to [a violent climax] by Hitler, a maniacal dictator."[190] He explains further:

This collective madness, this "running off the rails," is usually explained by [a] combination of . . . factors. . . . The greatest of these factors is Hitler's personality itself and [the way it affected] the German people. It is certain that his personal obsessions, his . . . hatred, his preaching of violence, [were echoed by] the frustrat[ed] . . . German people, and for this reason [proved] his delirious conviction that he himself was . . . the Superman redeemer of Germany.[191]

Germans of the 1920s and 1930s needed a scapegoat, someone to blame for their miserable state, as well as someone to raise them out of it. And so, when Adolf Hitler claimed that Jews and other "inferior" beings were responsible for their problems, the people were ready to believe him. There is no doubt that Hitler—along with millions of Germans—truly believed he was "the Superman redeemer of Germany." In his adopted homeland he found the perfect setting from which to launch the Third Reich and lead it to "such dizzy heights and to such a sorry end." Hitler was, says journalist William Shirer, "a person of undoubted, if evil, genius." Shirer adds:

It is true that he found in the German people . . . a natural instrument which he was able to shape to his own [evil] ends. But without Adolf Hitler, who [had] a demonic personality, a granite will, uncanny instincts, a cold ruthlessness, a remarkable intellect, a soaring imagination and . . . an amazing capacity to size up people and situations, there almost certainly would never have been a Third Reich.[192]

The combination of the right person in the right place at the right time created one of the most evil empires in the history of man. But Adolf Hitler was not the only person, nor was Germany the only place, nor the 1930s the only time, when such evil has taken root. There have been other

---

Was There Any Good at All in Adolf Hitler?

We like to believe that there is some good in everyone, and most historians agree that Adolf Hitler did have some truly exceptional qualities that could have made him positively *rather than* negatively *important in history. Alan Bullock, in* Adolf Hitler: A Study in Tyranny, *and Helmut Heiber, in* Adolf Hitler: A Short Biography, *describe some of those qualities.*

"To achieve what he did Hitler needed—and possessed—talents out of the ordinary . . . which amounted to political genius. . . . His abilities [included]: his mastery of [certain] factors in politics, his insight into the weaknesses of his opponents, his gift for simplification, his sense of timing, his willingness to take risks. . . . An opportunist . . . , he showed considerable consistency and . . . astonishing [willpower] in pursuing his aims. . . . The fact that his career ended in failure, and that his defeat was . . . due to his own mistakes, does not by itself detract from Hitler's claim to greatness."

"Hitler was an extremely skilful party leader, a crafty [rabble rouser], an inspiring speaker, and . . . something [must] even be said for him as a military leader. . . .

The system functioned on the whole [because of his] 'finger-tip feeling' for [practical] solutions.

One of Hitler's favorite projects [the autobahn] provided a communication network for military purposes [and] pointed the way to a technical future which at that time only few people were able to imagine. Here, thanks to Hitler's perhaps greatest talent—an [inborn] understanding of the technical problems—an unparalleled result was achieved."

Hitler speaks to thousands of fellow Nazis who helped make his evil plans a reality.

examples in history and, historians warn, a similar catastrophe will happen again unless we learn from our past.

Psychoanalyzing Adolf Hitler

Many analysts who have studied Adolf Hitler since his death say that his condition was pathological: his mind was diseased, and he suffered from mental illness. As examples, they mention his intense worry about germs and disease and his obsession with cleanliness. They point to his fear of horses and moonlight. Some who knew him say that he sucked his little finger when he got upset. "He ordered the massacre of the innocents," wrote history professor Robert G. L. Waite in Langer's analysis of Hitler, "but worried about the most humane way to cook lobsters. . . . He played childish guessing games, seeing how fast he could get dressed or how quickly his valet could tie his tie for him."[193]

Understanding Adolf Hitler's mind, says Waite, is the key to understanding Nazism, World War II, and the Holocaust:

In Hitler's case, knowing the personality is of the very essence. For the political system he established was dependent ultimately upon the power of his person, the [effectiveness] of his charisma. He *was* Nazism. . . . His personal whim became the law of the land; his will decided war or peace in the world. Seldom in the history of Western civilization since Jesus had so much depended on one man's personality.[194]

Like a demented Pied Piper, Adolf Hitler used the charm of his personality to lead an entire nation down a path of evil that they and their descendants would regret into eternity. Only after it was way too late did the German people at last begin to understand the terrible price they had paid for worshipping a madman. Many claimed not to have realized the extent of the horror that had been going on all around them. *Life* magazine photographer Margaret Bourke-White, who was sent to Germany to photograph the concentration camps at the end of the war, said she heard these words repeated "thousands of times," by citizens living in the towns around the

What Kept Hitler from Becoming Great?

Why would a man who could be called a genius become, instead, the world's symbol of evil? Historian Hugh Trevor-Roper offers an explanation in his essay "The Mind of Adolf Hitler," reprinted in George Stein's book Hitler: Great Lives Observed.

"'A man,' said Bishop Berkeley, 'who hath not much meditated upon God, the human mind and the [highest good] may possibly make a thriving earthworm but will most [certainly] make a sorry patriot and a sorry statesman.' Hitler was a patriot and statesman of this sorry kind. He never meditated on these things. No word he ever uttered even so much as touched the human spirit. . . . He did not know the meaning of humanity. Weakness he despised, and pity . . . he despised also. . . . And if he despised physical weakness he also, in others, hated moral strength.

Love meant nothing to him. . . . Children were to him merely the continually replaceable . . . material of conquest and colonization. . . . And as for the purpose of human life . . . it was for him merely that Germans should be masters of the world."

Without the softer human qualities, says Trevor-Roper, Adolf Hitler became "the coarsest, cruellest, least [noble] conquerer the world has ever known."

camps: "'We didn't know. We didn't know.'" But, says Bourke-White, "they did know."[195] Now, with Hitler dead, they were left to bear the burden of guilt for having looked the other way, for having done nothing to stop the murder of six million Jews and five million other innocent human beings, and for having started a war that nearly destroyed mankind.

For all time his legacy must stand as a warning to the world. For this reason if no other, Adolf Hitler must be considered important in history. The fact that he was able to rise to power at all should be a frightening lesson. We must learn from his example that it is possible in modern, civilized times, among supposedly civilized people, for evil to take root. Do we want the horror of the Holocaust, the devastation of a scorched earth, the never-ending sorrow of war to happen all over again? If we are to avoid these cancers on humankind, we must look carefully to our past; otherwise we, too, will be caught in the magical spell of some new and vile Pied Piper. Historian Robert Payne has studied Hitler's charisma, the charm that allowed him to overpower millions of people. And sadly, he concludes, we have not learned the lessons that we should from Adolf Hitler:

The bodies of Holocaust victims are exhumed from mass graves so they can be given a dignified burial.

So [complete] was his power that the German people . . . became little Hitlers masquerading in his shadow. He was their daily bread, their wine, and their dreams. . . . Even when he lied outrageously, and they knew he was lying, the Germans preferred to believe his lies rather than face the consequences of truth. . . .

The flames in the Chancellery garden are still burning, and Hitler is still alive. The Third Reich ended in utter horror and despair, but neither the Germans nor their enemies learned the lessons that should have been learned. The war against Hitler is still being fought, and there is as yet no sign of victory.[196]

The millions of dead soldiers on the battlefields, the millions of skeletons in the concentration camps, the millions of common citizens who lost their lives during World War II were not the only victims of Adolf Hitler's Third Reich. His empire of

misery lived on, long after April 30, 1945. The young people who survived the war or the concentration camps now faced a lifetime of guilt or sorrow, all because Adolf Hitler was allowed to come to power. Many of those people are still alive and carry with them the legacy of the führer. One is former Hitler Youth leader Alfons Heck, a seventeen-year-old German when Hitler died, now an American senior citizen:

> None of us who reached high rank in the Hitler Youth will ever totally shake the legacy of the *Führer*. . . . [For us] there will always be the memory of unsurpassed power, the intoxication of fanfares and flags proclaiming our new age. "Today, Germany belongs to us and tomorrow the world," we trumpeted in our anthem. We believed it. Tragically, now, we are the other part of the Holocaust, the generation burdened with the [evil] of Auschwitz. That is our life sentence, for we became the enthusiastic victims of our *Führer*.[197]

Notes

Introduction: "You, My Youth"

1. Alfons Heck, *A Child of Hitler*. Frederick, CO: Renaissance House, 1985, pp. 18-20.

2. Heck, *A Child of Hitler*, p. 24.

3. Heck, *A Child of Hitler*, p. 21.

4. Heck, *A Child of Hitler*, p. 22.

5. Quoted in Heck, *A Child of Hitler*, p. 23.

6. Quoted in Heck, *A Child of Hitler*, p. 16.

7. Otto Strasser, *Hitler and I*. Boston: Houghton Mifflin, 1940, p. 65.

8. George H. Stein, *Hitler: Great Lives Observed*. Englewood Cliffs, NJ: Prentice-Hall, 1968, p. 1.

9. Stein, *Hitler: Great Lives Observed*, p. iii.

Chapter 1: "In the House of My Parents"

10. Alan Bullock, *Hitler: A Study in Tyranny*. New York: Bantam Books, 1961, p. 2.

11. Bullock, *Hitler: A Study in Tyranny*, p. 2.

12. John Toland, *Adolf Hitler*. Garden City, NY: Doubleday, 1976, p. 5.

13. Toland, *Adolf Hitler*, p. 8.

14. Quoted in Toland, *Adolf Hitler*, p. 9.

15. Quoted in Toland, *Adolf Hitler*, p. 9.

16. Adolf Hitler, *Mein Kampf*. Boston: Houghton Mifflin, 1971, p. 8.

17. Eugene Davidson, *The Making of Adolf Hitler*. New York: Macmillan, 1977, p. 10.

18. Quoted in Toland, *Adolf Hitler*, p. 13.

19. Quoted in Toland, *Adolf Hitler*, p. 13.

20. Toland, *Adolf Hitler*, p. 15.

21. Quoted in Toland, *Adolf Hitler*, p. 15.

22. Hitler, *Mein Kampf*, p. 294.

23. Hitler, *Mein Kampf*, p. 17.

24. Hitler, *Mein Kampf*, p. 17.

Chapter 2: "The Most Miserable Time of My Life"

25. Quoted in Davidson, *The Making of Adolf Hitler*, p. 13.

26. Quoted in Toland, *Adolf Hitler*, p. 19.

27. Quoted in Robert Payne, *The Life and Death of Adolf Hitler*. New York: Praeger, 1973, p. 42.

28. Hitler, *Mein Kampf*, p. 18.

29. Payne, *The Life and Death of Adolf Hitler*, p. 45.

30. Quoted in Payne, *The Life and Death of Adolf Hitler*, p. 52.

31. Quoted in Payne, *The Life and Death of Adolf Hitler*, p. 53.

32. Quoted in Payne, *The Life and Death of Adolf Hitler*, p. 53.

33. Quoted in Payne, *The Life and Death of Adolf Hitler*, p. 50.

34. Quoted in Toland, *Adolf Hitler*, p. 29.

35. Quoted in Toland, *Adolf Hitler*, p. 41.

36. Quoted in Bullock, *Hitler*, p. 12.

37. Quoted in Bullock, *Hitler*, p. 12.

38. Quoted in Toland, *Adolf Hitler*, p. 48.

39. Hitler, *Mein Kampf*, p. 52.

40. Hitler, *Mein Kampf*, p. 59.

Chapter 3: "An Exceptionally Brave, Effective, and Conscientious Soldier"

41. Hitler, *Mein Kampf*, pp. 124, 126.

42. Quoted in Werner Maser, *Hitler's Letters and Notes*. New York: Harper & Row, 1973, p. 32.

43. Quoted in Maser, *Hitler's Letters and Notes*, pp. 32-33.

44. Quoted in Toland, *Adolf Hitler*, p. 60.

45. Quoted in Bullock, *Hitler*, p. 26.

46. Quoted in Maser, *Hitler's Letters and Notes*, p. 45.

47. Quoted in Maser, *Hitler's Letters and Notes*, pp. 53, 54, 57.

48. Quoted in Maser, *Hitler's Letters and Notes*, p. 67.

49. Quoted in Charles Bracelen Flood, *Hitler: The Path to Power*. Boston: Houghton Mifflin, 1989, pp. 25-26.

50. Quoted in Flood, *Hitler*, p. 19.

51. Quoted in Toland, *Adolf Hitler*, p. 74.

52. Hitler, *Mein Kampf*, p. 202.

53. Hitler, *Mein Kampf*, p. 202.

54. Quoted in Flood, *Hitler,* p. 58.

55. Quoted in Davidson, *The Making of Adolf Hitler,* p. 117.

56. Hitler, *Mein Kampf,* p. 206.

57. Quoted in Payne, *The Life and Death of Adolf Hitler,* p. 138.

58. Quoted in Payne, *The Life and Death of Adolf Hitler,* p. 131.

Chapter 4: "I Alone Bear the Responsibility"

59. Quoted in Payne, *The Life and Death of Adolf Hitler,* p. 145.

60. Quoted in Payne, *The Life and Death of Adolf Hitler,* p. 143.

61. Quoted in Payne, *The Life and Death of Adolf Hitler,* p. 143.

62. Toland, *Adolf Hitler,* p. 101.

63. Quoted in Toland, *Adolf Hitler,* p. 101.

64. Quoted in Payne, *The Life and Death of Adolf Hitler,* p. 153.

65. Quoted in Konrad Heiden, *A History of National Socialism.* London: Methuen, 1934, pp. 44-45.

66. Quoted in Toland, *Adolf Hitler,* p. 156.

67. Quoted in Bullock, *Hitler,* p. 79.

68. Quoted in Walter C. Langer, *The Mind of Adolf Hitler.* New York: Basic Books, 1972, p. 223.

69. Quoted in Bullock, *Hitler,* p. 88.

Chapter 5: The NSDAP Is Reborn

70. James Taylor and Warren Shaw, *The Third Reich Almanac.* New York: World Almanac, 1987, p. 198.

71. Flood, *Hitler,* p. 598.

72. Flood, *Hitler,* pp. 599-600.

73. Taylor and Shaw, *The Third Reich Almanac,* p. 305.

74. Hitler, *Mein Kampf,* p. 688.

75. Quoted in Langer, *The Mind of Adolf Hitler,* pp. 102, 103.

76. Quoted in Toland, *Adolf Hitler,* p. 268.

77. Quoted in Leonard Mosley, *The Reich Marshal: A Biography of Hermann Goering.* New York: Doubleday, 1974, p. 133.

78. Quoted in Stein, *Hitler,* p. 57.

79. Stein, *Hitler,* p. 55.

80. Quoted in Bullock, *Hitler,* pp. 184-185.

81. Toland, *Adolf Hitler,* p. 291.

82. Quoted in Toland, *Adolf Hitler,* p. 291.

83. Quoted in Toland, *Adolf Hitler,* p. 295.

84. Quoted in Toland, *Adolf Hitler,* p. 296.

Chapter 6: "Forward with God!"

85. Quoted in Toland, *Adolf Hitler,* p. 302.

86. Strasser, *Hitler and I,* p. 142.

87. Strasser, *Hitler and I,* p. 143.

88. Quoted in Davidson, *The Making of Adolf Hitler.* p. 363.

89. Strasser, *Hitler and I,* p. 143.

90. Quoted in Barbara Rogasky, *Smoke and Ashes: The Story of the Holocaust.* New York: Holiday House, 1988, p. 25.

91. Toland, *Adolf Hitler,* p. 345.

92. Quoted in Robert Goralski, *World War II Almanac: 1931-1945.* New York: Bonanza Books, 1984, p. 28.

93. Strasser, *Hitler and I,* p. 175.

94. Quoted in William L. Shirer, *The Rise and Fall of the Third Reich.* New York: Simon & Schuster, 1960, p. 227.

95. Sebastian Haffner, *The Meaning of Hitler.* New York: Macmillan, 1979, pp. 28-29.

96. Shirer, *The Rise and Fall of the Third Reich,* p. 233.

97. Hitler, *Mein Kampf,* pp. 327, 453.

98. Hitler, *Mein Kampf,* pp. 652-653.

Chapter 7: Certain Signs of War

99. William L. Shirer, *Berlin Diary.* New York: Knopf, 1941, pp. 49-50.

100. Shirer, *Berlin Diary,* pp. 55-56.

101. Quoted in Shirer, *Berlin Diary,* p. 53.

102. Bullock, *Hitler,* p. 320.

103. Quoted in Bullock, *Hitler,* p. 321.

104. Shirer, *Berlin Diary,* p. 95.

105. Taylor and Shaw, *The Third Reich Almanac,* p. 321.

106. Bullock, *Hitler,* p. 387.

107. Quoted in Goralski, *World War II Almanac*, p. 70.

108. Quoted in Goralski, *World War II Almanac*, p. 72.

109. Quoted in Shirer, *The Rise and Fall of the Third Reich*, pp. 430-431.

110. Quoted in Goralski, *World War II Almanac*, p. 84.

111. Quoted in Goralski, *World War II Almanac*, p. 87.

112. Quoted in Shirer, *The Rise and Fall of the Third Reich*, p. 532.

Chapter 8: "Today Germany, Tomorrow the World"

113. Bullock, *Hitler*, p. 435.

114. Quoted in Goralski, *World War II Almanac*, p. 90.

115. Quoted in Stein, *Hitler*, pp. 76-77.

116. Toland, *Adolf Hitler*, p. 674.

117. Shirer, *Berlin Diary*, p. 200.

118. Quoted in Joachim C. Fest, *Hitler*. New York: Harcourt Brace Jovanovich, 1974, p. 626.

119. Quoted in Fest, *Hitler*, p. 626.

120. Quoted in Maser, *Hitler's Letters and Notes*, p. 288.

121. Payne, *The Life and Death of Adolf Hitler*, pp. 382-383.

122. Quoted in Fred Taylor, ed., *The Goebbels Diaries: 1939–1941*. New York: Penguin Books, 1982, pp. 123-124.

123. Quoted in Goralski, *World War II Almanac*, p. 127.

124. Quoted in Goralski, *World War II Almanac*, p. 127.

125. Quoted in Payne, *The Life and Death of Adolf Hitler*, p. 405.

126. Quoted in Stein, *Hitler*, p. 79.

127. Quoted in Stein, *Hitler*, p. 79.

128. Quoted in Albert Speer, *Inside the Third Reich*. New York: Macmillan, 1970, p. 248.

129. Quoted in Goralski, *World War II Almanac*, p. 256.

130. Quoted in Taylor and Shaw, *The Third Reich Almanac*, p. 376.

131. Quoted in Goralski, *World War II Almanac*, p. 257.

132. Speer, *Inside the Third Reich*, p. 250.

133. Quoted in David Irving, ed., *The Secret Diaries of Hitler's Doctor*. New York: Macmillan, 1983, p. 111.

134. Quoted in Irving, *The Secret Diaries*, p. 10.

135. Quoted in Irving, *The Secret Diaries*, pp. 107, 115, 116.

136. Quoted in Irving, *The Secret Diaries*, pp. 25, 119.

137. Hitler, *Mein Kampf*, p. 327.

138. Quoted in Toland, *Adolf Hitler*, p. 863.

139. Raul Hilberg, *The Destruction of the European Jews*. New York: Holmes & Meier, 1985, p. 293.

140. Quoted in Toland, *Adolf Hitler*, p. 862.

141. Bullock, *Hitler*, p. 632.

Chapter 9: The Invasion of Festung Europa

142. Quoted in Bullock, *Hitler*, p. 636.

143. Quoted in Laddie Lucas, ed., *Wings of War*. New York: Macmillan, 1983, pp. 251-252.

144. Toland, *Adolf Hitler*, p. 852.

145. Quoted in Mosley, *The Reich Marshal*, p. 304.

146. Quoted in Mosley, *The Reich Marshal*, p. 304.

147. Payne, *The Life and Death of Adolf Hitler*, p. 489.

148. Quoted in Payne, *The Life and Death of Adolf Hitler*, p. 185.

149. Quoted in David Irving, *The Trail of the Fox*. New York: E.P. Dutton, 1977, pp. 370, 371.

150. Speer, *Inside the Third Reich*, pp. 354-355.

151. Bullock, *Hitler*, p. 668.

152. Quoted in Payne, *The Life and Death of Adolf Hitler*, p. 498.

153. Payne, *The Life and Death of Adolf Hitler*, p. 191.

154. Quoted in Taylor and Shaw, *The Third Reich Almanac*, p. 317.

155. Quoted in Shirer, *The Rise and Fall of the Third Reich*, p. 1031.

156. Quoted in Shirer, *The Rise and Fall of the Third Reich*, p. 1056.

157. Quoted in Shirer, *The Rise and Fall of the Third Reich*, p. 1069.

158. Shirer, *The Rise and Fall of the Third Reich*, p. 1069.

159. Correlli Barnett, ed., *Hitler's Generals*. New York: Grove Weidenfeld, 1988, p. 314.

160. Quoted in Payne, *The Life and Death of Adolf Hitler*, p. 519.

161. Heck, *A Child of Hitler*, p. 114.

162. Quoted in Taylor and Shaw, *The Third Reich Almanac*, p. 38.

163. Quoted in Speer, *Inside the Third Reich*, p. 415.

164. Quoted in Irving, *The Secret Diaries*, p. 257.

Chapter 10: "The Chief Is Dead"

165. Quoted in Jadwiga Bezwinska and Danuta Czech, eds., *KL Auschwitz Seen by the SS*. Oswiecim, Poland: Panstwowe Muzeum w Oswiecimiu, 1978, p. 196.

166. Quoted in Toland, *Adolf Hitler*, pp. 956, 957.

167. Quoted in Goralski, *World War II Almanac*, p. 384.

168. Quoted in John Toland, *The Last 100 Days*. New York: Random House, 1966, pp. 266-267.

169. Quoted in Speer, *Inside the Third Reich*, p. 562.

170. Quoted in Shirer, *The Rise and Fall of the Third Reich*, p. 1110.

171. Shirer, *The Rise and Fall of the Third Reich*, p. 1110.

172. Payne, *The Life and Death of Adolf Hitler*, p. 347.

173. Quoted in Pierre Galante and Eugene Silianoff, *Voices from the Bunker*. New York: G.P. Putnam's Sons, 1989, p. 140.

174. Quoted in Hugh Trevor-Roper, *The Last Days of Hitler*. London: Macmillan, 1979, p. 117.

175. Trevor-Roper, *The Last Days of Hitler*, p. 118.

176. Speer, *Inside the Third Reich*, p. 485.

177. Quoted in Trevor-Roper, *The Last Days of Hitler*, pp. 130-131.

178. Trevor-Roper, *The Last Days of Hitler*, p. 141.

179. Quoted in Goralski, *World War II Almanac*, p. 400.

180. Quoted in Stein, *Hitler*, p. 83.

181. Trevor-Roper, *The Last Days of Hitler*, p. 199.

182. Quoted in Toland, *The Last 100 Days*, p. 539.

183. Quoted in Stein, *Hitler*, p. 84.

184. Quoted in Trevor-Roper, *The Last Days of Hitler*, pp. 203, 205.

Chapter 11: The World Looks Back on Adolf Hitler

185. Trevor-Roper, *The Last Days of Hitler*, p. 230.

186. Trevor-Roper, *The Last Days of Hitler*, p. 231.

187. Trevor-Roper, *The Last Days of Hitler*, p. 240.

188. Quoted in Eleanor H. Ayer, *Cities at War: Berlin*. New York: New Discovery Books, 1992, pp. 12-13.

189. Bullock, *Hitler*, pp. 724-725.

190. Primo Levi, *Survival in Auschwitz* and *The Reawakening*. New York: Summit Books, 1985, p. 392.

191. Levi, *Survival in Auschwitz*, pp. 392-393.

192. Shirer, *The Rise and Fall of the Third Reich*, pp. 5-6.

193. Langer, *The Mind of Adolf Hitler*, pp. 245-246.

194. Langer, *The Mind of Adolf Hitler*, p. 248.

195. Margaret Bourke-White, *Portrait of Myself*. New York: Simon & Schuster, 1963, p. 258.

196. Payne, *The Life and Death of Adolf Hitler*, p. 569.

197. Heck, *A Child of Hitler*, pp. 206-207.

For Further Reading

Eleanor H. Ayer, *Cities at War: Berlin*. New York: New Discovery Books, 1992. An account of World War II and Adolf Hitler's rise to power from the perspective of teenagers living in Berlin in the 1930s and 1940s. For ages twelve to eighteen.

——, *Parallel Journeys*. New York: Atheneum Books for Children, 1995. The impact of Adolf Hitler on two survivors of his Third Reich: a Hitler Youth leader and a Jewish death camp survivor. For ages twelve to eighteen.

Edward F. Dolan Jr., *Adolf Hitler: A Portrait in Tyranny*. New York: Dodd Mead, 1981. An illustrated biography emphasizing how children were affected by the Third Reich. For ages twelve and older.

Ronald D. Gray, *Hitler*. Minneapolis, MN: Lerner Publications in conjunction with Cambridge University Press, 1981, 1983. An illustrated biography for older children and young adults.

Nathanial Harris, *Hitler*. Trafalgar, England: Batsford UK, 1989. A sixty-four page biography of Hitler from the British perspective. For grades seven through ten.

Bob Italia and Rosemary Wallner, eds., *Adolf Hitler*. Minneapolis, MN: Abdo & Daughters, 1990. A biography for grades four and up.

Judith Kerr, *When Hitler Stole Pink Rabbit*. New York: Dell, 1987. The impact of Hitler's rule on a child's life. For grades three and up.

Albert Marrin, *Hitler*. New York: Viking Kestrel, 1987. A 250-page illustrated biography with special focus on Hitler's early life. For ages ten through fourteen.

Barbara Rogasky, *Smoke and Ashes: The Story of the Holocaust*. New York: Holiday House, 1988. An illustrated history of the Holocaust, with much information on the Third Reich and its leaders. For older children and young adults.

William L. Shirer, *The Rise and Fall of Adolf Hitler*. New York: Random House, 1961. An illustrated biography by the American journalist who witnessed Hitler's rise to power firsthand while working as a reporter in Germany. Shirer, the author of *The Rise and Fall of the Third Reich*, is one of the most respected historians on Hitler and the Nazis. For ages ten and older.

Gail B. Stewart, *Hitler's Reich*. San Diego: Lucent Books, 1994. Documented with dozens of primary-source quotations and interesting facts normally found only in adult books on the subject. For grades six through nine.

Works Consulted

Correlli Barnett, *Hitler's Generals*. New York: Grove Weidenfeld, 1989. Portraits of the military leaders of the Third Reich.

Jadwiga Bezwinska and Danuta Czech, eds., *KL Auschwitz Seen by the SS*. Oswiecim, Poland: Panstwowe Muzeum w Oswiecimiu, 1978. Collection of documents written by three SS officers at the Auschwitz concentration camp.

Margaret Bourke-White, *Portrait of Myself*. New York: Simon & Schuster, 1963. Autobiography of the great *Life* magazine photographer.

Alan Bullock, *Hitler: A Study in Tyranny*. New York: Bantam Books, 1961. Considered by many authorities to be the best biography of Adolf Hitler.

Edouard Calic, ed., *Secret Conversations with Hitler*. New York: John Day Company, 1971. Two lengthy interviews with Hitler in 1931 by a German newspaperman.

Eugene Davidson, *The Making of Adolf Hitler*. New York: Macmillan 1977. Hitler's early life and rise to power, from 1889 to 1933.

Lucy S. Dawidowicz, *The War Against the Jews, 1933–1945*. New York: Bantam Books, 1976. A history of the Holocaust that presents both the German and Jewish sides.

Joachim C. Fest, *Hitler*. New York: Harcourt Brace Jovanovich, 1974. The prologue poses the question, "Ought we to call him 'great'?" It is followed by a thoroughly researched analytical biography, from childhood to death.

Charles Bracelen Flood, *Hitler: The Path to Power*. Boston: Houghton Mifflin, 1989. An in-depth look at the period of Hitler's political apprenticeship in the years immediately after World War I.

Pierre Galante and Eugene Silianoff, *Voices from the Bunker*. New York: G.P. Putnam's Sons, 1989. Hitler's last days, told by those who were with him in the bunker.

Robert Goralski, *World War II Almanac: 1931–1945*. New York: Bonanza Books, 1984. Day-by-day entries of all major events leading up to and through World War II.

Sebastian Haffner, *The Meaning of Hitler*. New York: Macmillan, 1979. Examines the mystery of Adolf Hitler: who he was, how he used his power, and why he was destined to fail.

Alfons Heck, *A Child of Hitler*. Frederick, CO: Renaissance House, 1985. Autobiography of a former high-ranking Hitler Youth leader.

Konrad Heiden, *A History of National Socialism*. London: Methuen, 1934. The birth and development of the NSDAP, published just one year after Hitler came to power.

Robert Edwin Herzstein, *The Nazis*. Alexandria, VA: Time-Life Books, 1980. A heavily illustrated history from the World War II series describing the men and the policies that controlled the Third Reich.

Raul Hilberg, *The Destruction of the European Jews*. New York: Holmes & Meier, 1985. Considered one of the finest histories of the Holocaust.

Adolf Hitler, *Mein Kampf*. Boston: Houghton Mifflin, 1971. Hitler's autobiographical plan for his takeover of Europe and destruction of the Jews.

David Irving, *The Trail of the Fox*. New York: E. P. Dutton, 1977. The military activities of the famous German general Erwin Rommel, the Desert Fox.

David Irving, ed., *The Secret Diaries of Hitler's Doctor*. New York: Macmillan, 1983. The journals of Theodor Morell, physician to Adolf Hitler.

Walter C. Langer, *The Mind of Adolf Hitler*. New York: Basic Books, 1972. The secret wartime psychological analysis of Hitler, done by a professional psychoanalyst.

Primo Levi, *Survival in Auschwitz* and *The Reawakening*. New York: Summit Books, 1985. Autobiographical account of an Italian Jewish Holocaust survivor.

Laddie Lucas, ed., *Wings of War*. New York: Macmillan, 1983. Airmen of all nations give accounts of their service in World War II.

Kurt G. W. Ludecke, *I Knew Hitler*. New York: Charles Scribner's Sons, 1937. Written by a Nazi who escaped the Röhm Purge, or Night of the Long Knives.

Werner Maser, *Hitler's Letters and Notes*. New York: Harper & Row, 1973. Collection of selected letters, notes, drawings, and documents by Hitler, many in his own handwriting.

Leonard Mosley, *The Reich Marshal: A Biography of Hermann Goering*. New York: Doubleday, 1974. Story of the number two man in the Third Reich, Hitler's closest associate and head of the Luftwaffe.

Robert Payne, *The Life and Death of Adolf Hitler*. New York: Praeger, 1973. One of the major biographies of Hitler, showing how a corrupt man achieved absolute power.

Gordon W. Prange, ed., *Hitler's Words, 1923–43*. Washington, DC: American Council on Public Affairs, 1944. Collection of selected speeches made by Hitler during these two decades.

William L. Shirer, *Berlin Diary*. New York: Knopf, 1941. Diary entries from an American journalist on assignment in Berlin from 1934 to 1941.

———, *The Rise and Fall of the Third Reich*. New York: Simon & Schuster, 1960. Considered by most to be the best comprehensive history of the Third Reich—twelve hundred pages of painstakingly documented, thoroughly researched material by a journalist who was an eyewitness to much of the history.

Albert Speer, *Inside the Third Reich*. New York: Macmillan, 1970. First-person account of the man who was at first the chief architect and later the head of arms production for Hitler's Reich.

George H. Stein, *Hitler: Great Lives Observed*. Englewood Cliffs, NJ: Prentice-Hall, 1968. A collection of observations on

Adolf Hitler by those who knew him or lived under his spell.

Otto Strasser, *Hitler and I.* Boston: Houghton Mifflin, 1940. A revealing look at Hitler by a former Nazi who turned into an outspoken opponent of National Socialism.

Fred Taylor, ed., *The Goebbels Diaries: 1939–1941.* New York: Penguin Books, 1982. Personal diaries of Hitler's minister of propaganda.

James Taylor and Warren Shaw, *The Third Reich Almanac.* New York: World Almanac, 1987. Encyclopedic entries of people, events, and places in the history of the Third Reich.

John Toland, *Adolf Hitler.* Garden City, NY: Doubleday, 1976. One of the best biographies of Hitler, by a Pulitzer Prize–winning author.

———, *The Last 100 Days.* New York: Random House, 1966. Interviews with more than six hundred people who served Hitler or helped to defeat him.

Hugh Trevor-Roper, *The Last Days of Hitler.* London: Macmillan, 1979. In-depth analysis of Hitler and the Third Reich from August 1944 to war's end, focusing especially on April 20 to May 1, 1945.

Elie Wiesel, *Night.* New York: Bantam Books, 1982. Autobiographical account of this teenage death camp survivor.

Index

"Ten Commandments of Lawful Self-Defense" against, 61
Jodl, Alfred, 73
Junge, Traudl, 102
Jungvolk, 10

Kahr, Gustav, 42
Kaltenbrunner, Ernst, 98-99
Keitel, Wilhelm, 74
Kristallnacht, 66-68
Kubizek, August, 22-23, 25-26, 98

The Last 100 Days (Toland), 96
Lebensraum, 63-64
  Kristallnacht and, 66-68
Ley, Robert, 60
The Life and Death of Adolf Hitler (Payne), 15, 47, 68, 93, 101
Locarno Pact, 62
Lochner, Louis, 47
loyalty oath, 59
Ludecke, Kurt G. W., 41
Ludendorff, Erich, 42-43, 54
Ludwig (king of Bavaria), 31

maps
  Europe
    in 1914, 29
    post-World War I, 34
  of German advances, 1939–1940, 76
May, Karl, 22
Mein Kampf (Hitler), 14
  quotations from, 19, 26, 35, 36, 61
  Volume I written in prison, 44-46
  Volume II published, 46

military activity, Hitler's (chronologically)
  before World War II, bloodless advances through
    Austria, 63-64
    Rhineland, 62-64
    Sudetenland, 66
    Czechoslovakia, remainder of, 68-69
  World War II
    occupation of Poland, 71-72
    occupation of Denmark and Norway, 74
    occupation of Netherlands and Belgium, 74-75
    occupation of France, 75
    Battle of Britain, 75-77
    invasion of Soviet Union, 77-79
    defeat near Leningrad, 79-80
    bombing of Hamburg, 86-89
    D day invasion, 88-89
    Allies recapture Paris, 94
    Battle of the Bulge, 95
    Russians advance from east, 97
    fall of Berlin, war ends, 106
The Mind of Adolf Hitler (Langer), 32, 39, 43
"The Mind of Adolf Hitler" (Trevor-Roper), 112
Morell, Theodor, 80, 82, 95
Mussolini, Benito, 88, 90, 92, 104
mustard gas, 33

National Socialist German Workers' Party. *See* Nazi Party
National Sozialistische Deutsche Arbeiter Partei. *See* Nazi Party
Nazi Party
  darker side of, 60-61
  growth of, 44-52
  requirements for membership in, 47
  rise to power, 54-57
Night of the Broken Glass (Kristallnacht), 66, 68
Night of the Long Knives, 57-58
Night (Wiesel), 97
NSDAP. *See* Nazi Party
Nuremberg Laws, 60-61

Operation Barbarossa, 77-78
Operation Sea Lion, 76-77

Paulus, Friedrich, 79-80
Polish Corridor, 69
"Political Testament" (Hitler), 103, 105
political tradition of Germans, as fatal, 108-109
Popp, Anna, 31-32
Pötsch, Leopold, 21
propaganda and terrorism, as power, 58, 75

racial purity, 61
Raeder, Erich, 76-77
Rath, Ernst vom, 66
Raubal, Geli, 47-48, 58
Reichsparteitag, 10
Reichswehr, 62, 64

Ribbentrop, Joachim von, 70

Rienzi (opera; Wagner), 22-24

The Rise and Fall of the Third Reich (Shirer), 24, 42, 58

Röhm, Ernst, 39, 44, 47
  eradicated as threat, 57

Rommel, Erwin, 83, 88-89, 91
  "suicide" of, 93

Roosevelt, Franklin D., 98-99

SA (Sturmabteilung/ Brownshirts)
  eradicated with Röhm, 58
  formed, 39
  function of, 39
  rapid growth of, 49, 57

Schicklgruber, Alois, Jr., 16-17

Schicklgruber, Angela, 16, 48

Schicklgruber, Marie Anna, 15

Schirach, Baldur von, 55

Schleicher, Kurt von, 52-53, 57

Schuschnigg, Kurt von, 63-64

Schutzstaffel. *See* SS

scorched-earth policy, 99

Secret Conversations with Hitler (Calic, ed.), 51, 56

Soviet Union
  German-Soviet (nonaggression) Pact, 70
    broken by Hitler, 78
  see also military activity

SS (Schutzstaffel)
  Death's Head Units, 70
  eradication of enemies, 57-58
  extermination of Jews, 84
  formation of, 46
  rapid growth of, 49

Stalin, Joseph, 70, 98

Stauffenberg, Claus von, 91-92

Stempfle, Bernhard, 58

Strasser, Gregor, 53
  eradication of, 57-58

Strasser, Otto, 12, 53-54, 57-58

Strength Through Joy program, 60

Sturmabteilung. *See* SA

Survival in Auschwitz (Levi), 109

"Ten Commandments of Lawful Self-Defense", 61

Third Reich, 12

Treaty of Versailles, 34, 38, 62

Tunnel (movie), 28-29

Untermenchen (subhumans), 65

Völkische Beobacter, 39

völkisch movement, 21

Volkswagen, 59-60

von Papen, Franz, 50-53

Wagner, Richard, 23-24

Waite, Robert G. L., 111

Wansee Conference, 83-84

The War Against the Jews (Dawidowicz), 61

Wehrmacht, 74, 78

Weimar Republic, 37, 40-41, 48

Wiesel, Elie, 97

Wilson, Woodrow, 34

Wolf's Lair, 80, 82, 92, 97

Yalta conference, 98

Picture Credits

Cover photo by UPI/Bettmann

Adolf Hitler: Bilder aus dem Leben des Fuhrers, Hamburg: Herausgegeben Vom Cigaretten, 1936/Courtesy of the Simon Wiesenthal Center Beit HaShoah Museum of Tolerance Library/Archives, Los Angeles, CA, 109.

AP/Wide World Photos, 22, 27 (top), 62

Archive Photos, 24, 60

Archive Photos/G.D. Hackett, 72 (top)

Archive Photos/Popperfoto, 44

Bet Lohame Ha—Geta'ot/Courtesy of the Simon Wiesenthal Center Beit HaShoah Museum of Tolerance Library/Archives, Los Angeles, CA, 66

The Bettmann Archive, 18, 50, 59

Bildarchiv Preussischer Kulterbesitz/ Courtesy of the Simon Wiesenthal Center Beit HaShoah Museum of Tolerance Library/Archives, Los Angeles, CA, 96

Dachau Concentration Camp Memorial/ Courtesy of the Simon Wiesenthal Center Beit HaShoah Museum of Tolerance Library/Archives, Los Angeles, CA, 85

*Deutschland Erwacht/*Courtesy of the Simon Wiesenthal Center Beit HaShoah Museum of Tolerance Library/Archives, Los Angeles, CA, 111

Library of Congress, 9, 11, 15, 16, 17, 37, 38, 40, 42, 43, 46, 48, 49, 65, 87, 98

National Archives, 10, 12, 13, 14, 31, 33 (both), 41, 52, 54, 55, 56, 57, 63, 72 (bottom), 74, 75, 77, 78, 79, 80, 81, 82, 83, 88, 89, 90, 91, 94, 95, 99, 100, 101, 105, 107, 113

UPI/Bettmann, 25, 27 (bottom), 69, 70, 86, 104, 106

© All rights reserved, Yad Vashem, 67

About the Author

Eleanor H. Ayer is the author of more than two dozen books for children and young adults, several of which deal with World War II and the Holocaust. Among them are *The United States Holocaust Memorial Museum*, and *Berlin* in the Cities at War series, and *Parallel Journeys*, the interwoven stories of a Jewish Holocaust survivor and a former Hitler Youth leader. Her other biographies include books on Russian president Boris Yeltsin, *Life* magazine photographer Margaret Bourke-White, and Supreme Court justice Ruth Bader Ginsburg.

Mrs. Ayer has a master's degree in literacy journalism from Syracuse University's Newhouse School of Journalism. The mother of two boys, she lives in Frederick, Colorado, where she and her husband operate a small book publishing company.